TRIALS AND TRIBULATIONS

Trials *and* Tribulations

How One Teen Mom Came
through Childhood Abuse
and Poverty to Manifest a
Million-Dollar Life

Atiyah Nichols

LIONCREST
PUBLISHING

TRIALS AND TRIBULATIONS

How One Teen Mom Came through Childhood Abuse and Poverty to Manifest a Million-Dollar Life

ISBN   978-1-5445-2041-4   *Paperback*
        978-1-5445-2040-7   *Ebook*

This book is dedicated to my late mother, my children, and my family.

When I was thirteen, Momma gave me Maya Angelou's book I Know Why the Caged Bird Sings to read. That book lifted a weight off my heart. It details the abuse Ms. Angelou suffered as a child, and how she overcame it while being raised by her grandmother. Her book showed me how important it can be to tell your story and to release your own shame so it cannot dwell in you anymore.

I wrote this memoir to release the shame that was brought into my life that I didn't ask for. Shame is like a virus, and it grows in secrecy. In her work studying shame, researcher and writer Dr. Brené Brown says shame is not able to thrive when empathy shows up to shut it down. A lot of us have to learn to have empathy for other people's stories.

I hope that reading my story blesses your life.

Contents

INTRODUCTION 9

1. THE BEGINNING 23

2. MY CHICAGO CHILDHOOD 41

3. TAKEN ADVANTAGE 71

4. STARTING OVER AND GOING BACKWARD 87

5. HOOD LIFE 97

6. TELLING MY TRUTH 111

7. KNOWING MY WORTH 125

8. TEEN MOM ON WELFARE 135

9. ENTREPRENEURSHIP 151

10. I BELIEVE IN THE SURVIVAL 165

11. THE VISION 173

CONCLUSION 183

Introduction

"When we deny our stories, they define us. When we own our stories, we get to write a brave new ending."

—DR. BRENÉ BROWN

Sometimes, I hear voices.

Since childhood they've come, unwelcome little thoughts left over from conversations with people who feel some kind of way about me. They rattle around, working an inside job, trying to knock me into line.

The first time I sat down to tell my story I heard the voices of all those friends and associates who over the years have looked at me and seen a mouthy little girl getting above herself.

"There goes Tiyah," they would say. "She sure thinks she's something."

It's been four years since I wrote the first draft of the introduction to my book. This time, as I sit down to take another stab at putting pen to paper, I'm not listening to their voices. I'm listening to my own voice, guided by God's hand on my back to make sure I'm headed in the right direction with this book. I still want you to hear some of what I had to say to those haters in my first draft. The little rebuttal that I wrote will give you a feel for what was on my mind during one of the hardest times of my life.

I called the introduction, *My Life from All Angles*. Here's a taste of what I wrote:

MY FIRST DRAFT

> I know you all are wondering: "What does this girl have to say about her life? What makes her story so special she had to write a book?"
>
> Or maybe: "Here she goes again, thinking she's better than everybody, living this fairy-tale life, so she's gonna write a book."
>
> Thirty-one years old, with only two kids (would have been three if all were living…a sensitive subject), my own business, owning three homes and counting, driving fine cars, in my second marriage with a husband who loves me unconditionally.

Coming from where I come from, I wasn't supposed to be here.

But my life is different from yours because it's mine. There's no two people completely alike. We might be similar, but we are not the same.

Where do I come from? Where should I start...

That was the feeling I had on me in the moment: a buildup of frustration from the energy people had been giving me my whole life, that who-do-you-think-you-are energy. And I'd had enough. I wanted to crush it for Atiyah and for every other woman who has been told she should expect less out of life, dream smaller.

Reading it back four years later, some of it sounds pretty snotty since I'm not in that space anymore. But it was real for me then.

Funny thing is even though those comments have come since I was little, and even though I admit I collected them and gave them a lasting space in my brain, I still always found them easy to dismiss in the past.

During every other stage of my life, no matter what trials I found myself going through, I had always known "who I think I am." I'm the daughter of a king, a blessed child of God, no doubt in my mind. I'm confident in God's plan for me.

The stretch of time right before I sat down to write that first draft of my book was different, though. I had lost my mom and a child back to back. And for the first time in my life, I didn't feel so confident in God's protection.

When you get deeper into this book, reading about the way I grew up, you might find it hard to believe that during all of my struggles I had considered myself favored by God. But that's the point: In the past, the things that happened to me couldn't keep me down because my faith in God's love made me untouchable.

ALONE FOR THE FIRST TIME

Four years ago, though, two things changed. First, I lost my mom. I was devastated and exhausted and threw myself into overworking. All I wanted was to keep moving, keep going, to avoid sitting with what I was feeling.

Not dealing with my emotions didn't work, though; it simply stoked my anxiety. Now that I knew I could lose someone, I wondered: Was there no end to what else could be stolen from me? Was I still under God's protection at all? Or was I now completely vulnerable? I felt scared of losing the business, my kids, dropping the ball, and not being a good mother.

At work, I felt like I had to do everything myself. I couldn't leave a single thing in someone else's hands. If you were watching me from the outside during that time, it probably seemed like I thought I had everything in the bag. But it wasn't that. I was lost, heartbroken, and terrified about what was going to happen next. And the only way I could hold it together was to be in complete control.

With my mom's death, everyday life had changed for everyone in my household. I wasn't one to sit on the phone for hours gossiping with my mom. But she was still a daily touchstone. Most days I would stop by her house to say hey. My kids' daily lives were altered, too, now that they had lost their Nandi. Thanks to my mom, I had never needed to put them in daycare. Instead, they spent their days in her loving care.

After she died, my son became quiet for a while, missing everything that he was used to getting from Nandi. These weren't material things; she was always letting him know she loved him, feeding him physically and spiritually. I didn't know how to see him through that sadness. And I didn't know how to express my own emotions. The only thing I knew how to do was enact tunnel vision and focus on work. So that's what I did.

I mean, I tried to help my son. I told him, "Nandi is looking over you." But I knew I needed to say more. The ground had shifted in my home, and I didn't know how to make it okay for myself, let alone my little ones.

Then, my husband and I found out we were expecting. I

believed God had sent me a child as a blessing to help me through. A baby wouldn't make us stop missing Momma, but knowing we were pregnant lifted our spirits. The news had everyone in our house remembering how to smile again. The little ones stopped dragging themselves around weeping about Nandi long enough to rub my belly.

In the midst of that storm God had brought something back to us, I thought. Some people lose their minds going through a loss like this, but God needs us to make it through. He needs us to be warriors for him so that we can tell others how we made it through, I reasoned. So, He sent us this blessing.

The second hit arrived when our miracle baby was stillborn. The loss was overwhelming. This precious gift had been dangled right in front of us as a cure for our pain, only to be torn away and leave behind a layer of agony like I'd never felt before.

Life often plays cruel jokes on us: One person in my life had been perfectly suited to help me through my child's death. My mom had lost a baby before I was born. I grew up mourning the sister I never met, raised to think about her, talk to her. Momma had gotten through her pain and made it safe for my siblings and me to mourn. Now I desperately needed her to teach me how to do both of those things. But she was gone.

The pregnancy had promised joy and purpose to pull me through. Instead, it was gutting me and then making the first loss start its attack on my heart all over again.

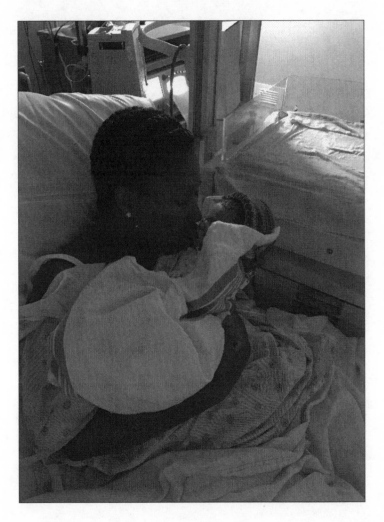

Drowning in pain, I felt my shield start to slip. The world had hurt me before, but those wounds were superficial because my faith had protected me; it was my armor. But these new wounds were deeper. And for the first time I felt the pain of women like me all around the world. I was one of them now asking, *Why, God, why?* I could never have imagined that my mom and my child would be taken away from me in one fell swoop. I couldn't accept that this torture was part of a plan.

This was deliberate? God wanted me to feel this way? My faith had always been strong. But I felt it crumbling in the face of being asked to believe that God would design my life to unfold like this.

I'm not sure how long I sat with this fresh suffering. It was long enough, though, that I'll never forget that feeling of connection to the universe of pain that exists in our world. I was wired into every woman and girl who felt hopeless because she had lost a child, had been hurt by a man, let down by the people who should have protected her, or made to feel ashamed of where she had been.

It felt terrible. I waded in the waters of all that pain for a while, walking in it and feeling every raw bit. At some point I got in deep enough to glimpse the line where my pain ended, and the world's hopelessness began. I could also now see the difference. Miles underwater I was hitting upon the bedrock of my faith, those reserves that Momma had carefully built up in all eleven of her living children. My disbelief and misery were outmatched when they hit up against that core. It was still there, washed in grief and anger and doubt, but still there. And little by little I moved back to myself. I slowly felt positivity and hope seeping back up to the surface.

Maybe I could mourn these horrific changes while still trusting God. Could I cry and yell and rage, but do some of that on my knees in prayer?

I started to feel like I could. Then I started to feel like I had to.

When my spiritual armor slipped, it showed me how other women—those without hope at their center—were suffering. Now that I had felt it, I wasn't ever going to be able to un-feel it. I was called to help. If I shared my story, would it inspire them? I could talk about the hope I hold inside and maybe teach them how to find that within themselves. I needed to write my book.

THIS BOOK IS FOR YOU

You know those voices we were talking about? Well, no doubt every one of those naysayers who originated them will be quick to ask me why I wrote a book when they find out I have.

But they won't be listening for my answer. Instead, they'll still be thinking they know me better than I know myself. In truth, they'll tell on themselves by assuming that the reasons that *they* might write a book—to bring glory to their accomplishments, to make the haters jealous, or to gain fame and more riches—are the reasons I have.

I can assure you, none of those are why I wrote this book.

I'm writing this book for you. I want to take you on the journey I've been on, show you how God protected me through my tribulations, and then bring you with me as He delivered me into this incredible life that I asked Him for.

You were in my heart as I wrote this book. If you need to find hope that life is good and can be glorious, especially if you're holding a secret that you haven't dealt with and it's preventing you from reaching your full potential, I can help because I've been there. I'm going to show you how. By talking about the secret you're holding, you will be able to be more present in your own life, focus on your family, and identify and follow your passion.

By the end of this book, I want to have given you some of the gifts I've been blessed with. I want you to understand the therapeutic benefits of sharing your story with someone in your life, how releasing your secrets can help you find your voice, how discussions with your children can lay the groundwork for trust and protect them into adulthood, how not to lose your faith because of the echoes of trauma, why you may have to remove yourself from your current situations to blossom, the way to connect to God and ask for His help, and how to stop chasing success that is meant for others so you can instead go after your own unique rewards.

I'm gonna tell you the truth, though, too. This book isn't for you if you want permission to use what you've been through as an excuse not to grow or as a pass to wallow in negativity. I'm not going to give you that. We're not handing out any passes today. So, if you're not ready for a transition, put the book down.

I wrote this book for every woman who wants to be uplifted, make a spiritual connection, and improve her marriage, parenting, career, and finances while also accessing gratitude for the lifestyle she's already been blessed with.

REWRITING MY ENDING

I'm the latest in a long line of women who didn't grow up in the same house as her own father or raise all their children with their fathers. I was a child of poverty and abuse and became a mother myself as a teenager. There are always going to be people who think that these facts mean that maybe I'm not entitled to ask for much out of my life.

But I'm going to keep asking anyway. I've learned that's how good things come to me. I asked God for the life I lead today: for healthy kids, a rock-solid marriage to safeguard them, and a financial legacy to secure their future. God heard me, saw that I had made space for Him, and came right in and changed my life.

I've also learned since I wrote the first draft of this book four years ago that the purpose of writing it isn't a public callout to the haters who thought I was too big for my britches since I was in diapers. I still wanted you to read that original intro I wrote, but now I want to tell you that today I'm not so focused on how we're different. Because you and I are the same.

Sure, maybe your brother didn't have to provide backup against the rats in the house you grew up in just so you could make it to the bathroom to pee in the middle of the night. But I know that our stories are still similar enough. I know that right now you're going through something that's got you feeling weary. I'm not sure precisely what it is—whether you've just gotten a scary diagnosis or he's hit you for the first or fifth time or you've made a mistake you think means now you're unworthy of a good life—but I know how it feels.

The difference is I've got something to hold tight to in my darkest moments. And I want you to have it, too. I've seen a lot of what can be wrong in life, but the grace of God has always been there if I looked for it and allowed Him in. I'm telling you: You may never have prayed a day in your life, but you can still invite God to help you.

As you read my story, that's the feeling I want you to get. You're going to hear about me and my brothers and sisters going without, feeling less than. You're going to hear about hood life and some messed-up relationships and about me being molested as a child. It's some darkness, sure. But I want you to see the light in my story, too.

As I'm introducing you to my siblings, to this family of mine living in poverty, to our challenges, I want to show you how God carried me. Because then you'll receive the best news you might ever hear: That He's also ready to lift you up just the same.

Should we get started?

CHAPTER 1

The Beginning

"There's nothing in the world in a woman's heart like her daddy's love. And if you don't have your daddy's love, not only will you continue to look for it in all the wrong places, you will sacrifice yourself to get it."

—IYANLA VANZANT

"Wow; that's a lot of kids. Did you all get along?"

That question, or some version of it, is the one I usually get as soon as someone hears I'm my mother's twelfth-born child. What was my home life like with that many kids they want to know. Was it amazing to have all those playmates, or did we drive each other nuts? Were we well behaved, or were we always in trouble?

Yes to all, depending on the day. That's the answer.

My family was pretty well established by the time I came into this world on July 1, 1985, with seven brothers and four sisters preceding me. Like all eleven of the other babies born to Ms. Hattie Smith, I arrived in Chicago, Illinois. My mother's third child had died tragically in infancy, so only ten children waited that summer to welcome their little sister.

I was born into a God-loving, funny, tight-knit family where I never lacked for a playmate or caregiver. My mom's final four children—including me—had been born one every two years. First came Jackson, then two years later Daniel, two years later Bronson, and then two years later, little, old me. We four grew up as our own little pod within the larger sibling bunch. I would make neighborhood friends, church friends, and school friends eventually. But these three were all I needed in my younger years, my first and best play-mates. We spent hours upon hours playing "friends" (our version of house), dancing, singing, and creating. And, thanks to all that togetherness, we also got at each other's throats.

So yeah, we fought. And when we fought, Momma would let it play out. She allowed us to establish, or test, our pecking order. Then, when the fight was over, discipline came next. Momma would let the fight come to its natural end, but she still wanted us to know we shouldn't have put hands on our own brother or sister in the first place. Both kids involved got a serious whooping. By the time the belt finished flying (or should I say twelve-piece stanching cord) we had forgotten we were enemies. We were back to brother and sister, partners in crime, except now we were comforting each other over the whooping we had just taken.

If the culprits were Bronson and me, we would scramble—noses running and tears streaming—up onto the sofa and collapse into each other's arms. There we would stay until our little chests stopped being wracked by sobs. In the meantime, we would sing quietly together, in between the lingering cries, because Momma had told us that's what we were supposed to do. Since I've been grown, I've learned that my older brothers and sisters had been required to do the same; Momma made them sit and sing "You Are My Sunshine" until they forgot what originally made them mad.

The lesson Momma wanted us to learn with those whoopings was that we are in this life together; you help your siblings. If one of you is in a fight you are all in a fight. If your sister or brother is in trouble, then you are all in trouble. That's how she raised us. Our household, all throughout my childhood, was chaotic. But this truth was constant: we took care of each other. If we were down to our last box of cereal, everybody got a bit of what was left. If the milk was almost out, we spread it across all the bowls, then added water as needed.

We were very much one big family, even though only those three youngest siblings shared a dad with me. Before that last set of four kids, Momma had given birth to twins. Ledosha was one of the twins, and the closest sister to me in age. The other twin was Charles, but I can't help but introduce him as Elder Charles from the jump, since he was born as every bit the preacher that he would eventually grow into as an adult. He also saved my life, as you'll learn in a later chapter.

Precious came before the twins, named for Momma's mom. Doeboy, the big brother who scared me most as I was coming up, came along before her. Hardy was my mom's fourth, her rainbow child who arrived after the family had lost my older sister Princess to crib death. Before Princess came Bryson, and Cookie was the oldest. Seven boys and five girls in all to Ms. Hattie, and she loved everyone.

MEN OF OUR HOUSE

When you come on the scene as the youngest of twelve, your family has lived a lot of life before you get there. The way our family worked, though, I never felt like I had missed out. I heard all the stories, saw all the emotions on the faces of my siblings and my mom to the point where it felt like I had gone through those earlier times right along with them.

The tale of my sister dying, for instance, was decades old by the time I was born, but it was real and present for me. I prayed to my sister Princess daily; I felt like I knew her. And I understood all of the details of what Momma had gone through when she lost her. Nineteen-year-old Hattie was the mother of three when her tiny, precious daughter one day simply stopped breathing. She went into a deep depression, stopped eating almost entirely, and shrunk down to an emaciated ninety pounds before prayer and the needs of her two living children brought her back.

And then there were the men of the house that came before I was born. Momma's household had known four fathers before my own dad entered the picture. And their histories with my mom were part of the legacy I was born into. Only one father was in residence by July of 1985, though. And, with all due respect to my siblings' dads, he was the very best of the bunch.

Marion Smith was mostly Smitty or Dee to us kids, and I

thought he was Superman. You couldn't tell me nothing about my dad when I was a little girl; I adored him without conditions.

If you've ever watched the show *Amen* from the late '80s then I can give you a vivid picture of Smitty. On *Amen*, Sherman Hemsley, who had been George on *The Jeffersons*, played a lawyer who was a deacon in his church. His character was always dapper and had this memorable walk. It was exaggerated and suave, and was 100 percent my dad's. Seriously, when my sisters and brothers and I first saw that show we were like: "That's my Dee! That's his same cool strut!"

The way Dee spoke was cool, too. He had this habit of dragging out his words, making each one last. His personal style came out in his clothes, too. Dee always looked nice, stepping out in crisp khakis and button-ups when other fathers in our neighborhood were usually so casual.

As a six-year-old, seeing my dad drive up to our house was one of my favorite things.

He'd be coming to collect my brothers and me for a visit, and we would be so excited as we waited for him to get there. If I close my eyes, I can still picture everything about those moments, right down to the smell of whatever he was driving that week. Dee was a car salesman at a dealership, so he was always switching out his ride. Everyone was shinier and cleaner than the last. Everyone was fresh enough that it still had that new car smell, and the paper mats would be lying on the floor, crinkling under our feet as we climbed in.

You know what's crazy, though? Those are my earliest clear memories of my dad.

Now you tell me: How did Dee live in our house for the first half decade of my life, yet it's not until age six that my real recollections of him start? I guess maybe something about the household split woke me up to making solid memories of him. Because after he and Momma broke up, I made plenty, and they aren't fuzzy at all.

Mostly, those memories are of Dee being really sweet to me. Whenever I would see him, it was all "baby girl," and him laughing at things I did wrong. Clearly, I was special to him, because when the boys did something wrong while we were visiting it was a different scene. Dee would get on them about whatever mistake they had made. With me, though, it was, "Oh, baby girl, you can't do that." He would have a smile on his face while he said it, and I always got the inkling that whatever he was trying to scold me about was actually okay with him.

WHO IS MY DEE?

My dad got the nickname Smitty because of his last name,

Smith. He got the name Dee when my older brother couldn't say, "Daddy" as a baby. Those two nicknames followed him as Momma bore him children number two, three, and four. By the time my parents broke up, his four babies were six, eight, ten, and twelve, all still calling him Dee. My older siblings, the ones who weren't biologically Smitty's, used the nickname, too. But it turned out they weren't saying it with as much fondness as I was.

See, I would later learn that there was some stuff I missed even after I was born. I might technically have been around during many of the years that Dee lived at home, but I was still too young to grasp the darker side of our household. Unlike the other family legends that my siblings and my mom filled me in on, they didn't get me up to speed on how Dee treated the older kids. I mean, I was there, after all. How were they supposed to know that I wasn't really forming memories of it all? I had no picture of how hard it was for them to be teenagers under his rule. Then, after the split, it was just the four of us who took visits to Dee's house. So, I rarely saw them interact. And by the time I was a teen myself, Dee had long since started to disappear from our lives.

Once I was grown, though, my brothers and sisters shared their stories of Dee during those early years. They talked about how quick Dee had been with his belt. And they told me about resenting him so much that they remember times when they silently plotted how they might come back as adults for revenge.

"Your daddy used to whip us like crazy," my older brothers and sisters told me. "If we came home from school with a test where we got one problem wrong, he would tear us up. We promised each other that when we got older, we were going to kill him."

By the time they were painting these pictures for me, though, they better understood his intentions, even if they still disapproved of his methods.

"Tiyah, he was just trying to keep us off the streets," my brother said. "He knew what the streets had for us. He knew the kind of people we were going to make friends with because we didn't have a choice. Those were the only friends on the block half the time. So, he knew he had to be scarier than the streets and those friends. He looked at it as training."

My six-year-old impression of Dee, though, held none of that. My dad hadn't yet started to disappoint me, so I still got to see him through a daughter's rose-colored glasses. There was a lot I was blind to. Some of it was serious, but some of it was pretty funny. Case in point: what I thought about the place Dee moved into after the breakup.

MOVING ON...UP?

When my dad moved out, my brothers and I kind of thought Dee had suddenly made it big. There's some sense to it when you look at the whole picture through our little-kid eyes. Our dad was already this sharp-dressed guy who was always driving a beautiful new car. Then Momma kicked him out and in no time, he had a new house of his own. This was a large single-family house with a great big yard. We would go to his new place and just be so impressed.

There were some signs that something was off with Dee's new house, but I missed every one of 'em. To start with, all four of us kids, plus Dee, would pile into one bedroom to sleep. Who knows how many rooms this big house had? But every visit we all jammed into one room when bedtime came. Given how many of us there were sharing space at home, though, I thought nothing of it. Or maybe I figured Dee just liked all of us all being together.

Then there was the bathroom situation. The bath we used in the hall near his room was clearly one that he shared. And he wasn't the only one using the kitchen, either. In fact, strangers were likely to show up in any part of the house outside of Dee's bedroom. None of that dulled the shine of his fancy new living situation for us, though.

As someone who today owns a number of group-living facilities, I have to laugh at what my siblings and I thought.

You guys, that wasn't his house!

Dee hadn't rebounded from the house that he and my mom had shared into a lovely single-family home. No, he had downgraded to renting a spot in a rooming house. We were all sharing a bedroom because that's the only part of the house that wasn't communal space.

There's honestly no shame in that. But when I compare what we thought his new living situation was to what I now know as an adult was probably going on, it's just silly. I loved Dee so much; he was my cool and stylish dad. So, I just saw his new home through that filter.

My older siblings didn't have the luxury of that filter, though, because they had long since seen how good my Dee was at disappointing the people who counted on him. It wasn't just the quick temper and aggressive discipline that had let them down. It was the fact that he was one more father figure who hadn't stuck around, who hadn't been a loyal partner to my mom, and who ultimately had offered some taste of a two-parent home only to rip it away with more pain than if it had never been dangled in front of them in the first place.

Think of how many times my oldest brother and sister, for instance, had seen the man of their house turn over. With each of Momma's successive marriages they didn't get a new father, because their own dad was still in their lives. But they got a new parental figure, a person to be listened to and pre-sumably trusted. And then one by one they lost that member of the household, and with each loss a little more of their stability went, too.

Each time, though, our family—the unit made up of my mom and her children—stayed intact, remained solid. Or maybe it grew stronger through each tribulation we went through together. Now, as an adult, I see that none of these men were true partners to my mom. Behind the scenes, she always held the whole weight of caring for the family on her shoulders. This seemed normal to me as a young child. And normal even to my older siblings. But it isn't, and she deserved more.

The bulk of my memories, of course, don't even start until Momma was a single parent again for the last time. As I remember it for my entire childhood, she was running her own show, feeding, educating, and keeping clothes on whatever selection of kids still lived at home at any given moment—plus the ones who were home again for a while.

That makes it a little weird for me to picture a day when Dee still lived at home with us all. Much later, I asked my mom to fill me in on what happened to break them up. There was no harm in telling me the whole story at that point, I'm sure she reasoned, because by then Dee had stopped coming around. What harm would it do for me to know the ugly truth of what had finally made her kick him out.

When I was born, Dee was still holding down a full-time job and respecting his marriage, at least as far as anyone knew. But by the time I started kindergarten things were getting rocky on both the work and marriage fronts. Dee had gradually been pulling back from family life, slinking out of the house more and more frequently to spend time with friends.

The house we stayed in then was on Claremont Street in Chicago. It was the last house that they lived in together, a one-story, single-family that I remember as being dark-brown brick. There was a detached garage in the back, and in the front, a little porch and almost no yard.

Here in the residential neighborhoods of Milwaukee, where I live today, there are small hills in front of our houses that roll down toward the sidewalk and then the street. It gives you a yard and a bit of separation between your front door and the curb. But in the part of Chicago, we lived in with Dee, the front yards were nonexistent. You walked out your front door and boom, you're on the sidewalk. It set up a weird kind of feeling, like you were always only one foot away from what was happening out on the streets. And nothing good was happening out on those streets.

The gangs were out of control back then in Chicago, and on our block in particular. If you were a young guy in that neighborhood, you were either in a gang, or you were trying to look like you were. Because it wasn't an option to just say,

"No thanks, I'm good, gangs aren't for me, but you do you. Have a good one, now." Your choice was either join or get jumped on every day. Most were too scared not to join; so, the numbers kept growing. And gang activity during the years I lived in Chicago kept rising.

I never understood it. I would swing open the front door of that house and look at everyone out there trying to be tough; it was nothing but stupid to me. As a child it all seemed so pointless to me, and my opinion hasn't changed in adulthood.

Not everyone in my house felt that way. After we moved to the other side of Chicago, one of my brothers wouldn't be able to quit hanging out with the friends he had made on Claremont. He would end up getting shot in that neighborhood two different times. Thank God, he lived to tell the tales. Years later, his son, my nephew, Tae, was not as lucky. He was shot and killed at a gas station in that same area. It was like a tragic circle was drawn around that neighborhood. My mom would say, "That area just wasn't no good for nobody."

Before any of those shootings took place, though, Claremont was already a place where my parents could no longer keep their peace. That garage out back became Dee's hideaway, where he entertained friends and blew off steam. It got so that he went straight out behind the house as soon as he came home. Inside the house, Momma was cooking, cleaning, parenting, paying bills, figuring out her own work schedule, and then making sure she had childcare coverage during any times she would be gone.

At night, after she got us all off to bed, she would sit on the little front porch and hear the music coming from back behind the house. The garage was bumping, the laughs were drifting up front, with the sounds of other people having a heck of a time on her property. Meanwhile she sat and worried about the family inside the house. And probably fumed a bit.

"Your dad would be smoking sherms back there," she told me, talking about cigarettes that are half weed and half tobacco, and then sometimes dipped in something a lot stronger. "He would come home from work and go right back to that garage with his friends."

She wanted no part of what was going on back there, Momma said, "I just got so tired of them coming over and partying like that."

Then came the day that one of Dee's friends put the final nail in his coffin. This pal came up front to say hello to Momma and for some reason decided to mention to her, "Women are going back there, you know?" She had probably known that, but it hadn't been thrown in her face until then.

"I just couldn't do it anymore," she admitted to me. "You know, you were born at this point. I had given birth to twelve kids. I was tired of fighting and arguing with him. You don't know how much your dad and I used to argue and fight. Now, not only was he not helping, but he was shaming our family. So, I told him to get out."

That's where Momma's story stopped. But it wasn't the actual end of the tale. I got the extended, uncut version from my brothers and sisters. They said that on this particular night, when Dee finally made his way back up to the house after his party broke up, Momma was waiting and confronted him about the women and then brought up the drugs, the music, the bills, and whatever other grievances had been building up. She had just hit her limit. Momma told Dee to get out—just like she had said in her retelling. But she had left out the fact that he wasn't trying to move out right away or give up on her that easily. So, when he didn't move fast enough to follow orders, she chased Dee off the property wielding a hammer. Then she followed behind him all through the neighborhood as he beat his retreat for good measure.

It made sense to her, as a woman and a wife, that her marriage was now over. But as Dee's children, we didn't understand why he was gone. He just disappeared on us and that hurt us all so much. First, he was suddenly absent from our house, but at least he would come to take us four biological kids for weekend visits. Pretty soon, though, the visits stopped. And then he was gone from our lives altogether in pretty much every way that mattered.

When the visits just stopped, we were confused. We so loved our dad. Even after he no longer lived with us, one of my brothers and I would sit on the couch when my mom went out to work nights and sing this little song that we had made up: "I want my Momma. I want my Dee. I want my Momma. I want my Dee."

We would rock back and forth, squeaking the springs on the couch, and singing it over and over. Dee never knew about that song. He was long gone, not knowing (and maybe not caring) how much he was missed by these little people who had counted on him always being around for them. Even while he was still collecting us for visits it became clear quickly that we couldn't count on him anymore. Dee would just pick and choose when he wanted to show up. It's not like we were completely out of touch, but Dee became distant. We had to force him to even come around. He missed so much.

From the outside you might say, "Yeah, but Tiyah, he was around for the big stuff, wasn't he? Give him credit for showing up for your high school graduation. Didn't he even walk you down the aisle at your first wedding?"

He did because my brother made him come. Would you believe that my brother had to go get him from Chicago, drive him here to Wisconsin, all to make sure I got a father to give me away? He just told him, "You're not missing it. I'm not letting you." My brother is kind of the glue for our family where Dee is concerned. He's spent the last few decades making sure we stay connected to our dad, even if Dee wasn't really earning it.

We loved my dad like crazy, and we felt the loss when he pulled away from us, but that didn't change the way I felt about our home. As I said, I don't really remember my home life when Dee lived with us. So, a home without Dee was always still a complete home to me. I had Momma, who I knew would always take care of me, the best playmates ever in my youngest brothers, and extra mothers and fathers in the form of my older siblings.

I didn't notice my mom pining for having a husband in the house either. It just wasn't out of the norm for her. He was hardly the first man who gave her children and then gave her trouble. And the cycle of a mother not living with the father of her children didn't start with Momma. When she told him to move out and then went on back to being the sole head of our household, she was only doing what she learned from her own family experiences growing up. It was all I remember. It was all she knew. And it certainly wasn't uncommon in the neighborhood we lived in.

CHAPTER 2

My Chicago Childhood

"We delight in the beauty of the butterfly, but rarely admit the changes it has gone through to achieve that beauty."

—MAYA ANGELOU

You might read a story or two in the newspaper about gang violence today in Chicago and shake your head. But if you could only imagine the crime, the killings, going on in 1991, 1992, and 1993 it might keep you up nights. Add in a fatherless household where the mother lives alone with her children, and you could get the impression that we weren't safe. I can tell you that it didn't feel that way to six-year-old me. I was being raised in faith by my mom and my grandmother, so I always sensed God's protection around me. But the first line of defense I counted on was

Momma. I never knew anyone to mess with Momma twice. She was a force to be reckoned with, even for these little drug dealers and gangsters who normally had no respect for anyone.

I remember the day I knew for sure that there was nothing my mother would not handle to keep my siblings and me safe.

The neighborhood lowlifes tried to make every young boy take part in their lifestyle. My brothers were no exception; the ones who were old enough were on the gangbangers' radar; they were constantly pressuring them and harassing them to join in. My older brother Doeboy knew it was happening and he had laid down the law within our family; he told the younger kids, "You can't go join any type of gang. It's not for you. If they ask you when I'm not with you, you just tell them that. You mention who your brother is and that I told you it's not something you can do."

Mind you, he was in one.

But he also knew it wasn't the way he wanted his little brothers to go, and he had said as much to the gang members who came up and bothered my brothers and him. That might seem hypocritical, but thinking back maybe it was his way of getting in with that element so that he would have some pull when he said that our family was off-limits. The message was mostly received. It didn't stop gang members from talking to my other brothers altogether, but I'm not sure any of us thought they were in real daily danger.

And then one day, that changed. Just the youngest four of us, Jackson, Daniel, Bronson, and I, walked to school together. That afternoon, for some reason, Jackson came home on his own, and wouldn't you know that those same hellions happened upon him. Or heck, maybe they planned it. I don't know. But Jackson learned real fast that they had decided that, at twelve, he was old enough to either be one of them or a target of their gang. They just jumped him and they beat the living crap out of him right there in broad daylight on a weekday afternoon.

I was terrified when he came into the house bloodied up. Jackson was my heart; this was my brother who, no matter how nappy my head was looking on any given day or how dingy my clothes were, would throw me on his back and take me with him if I wanted to tag along with him and his friends. He was always proud to claim me as his sister. If the other two brothers were picking on me, Jackson would be the one who said, "Man, leave her alone, you guys."

I felt such sorrow on me that day when he came home after being jumped. I cried like a baby. He was bloody and just looked like he had been taken apart. I couldn't tell how bad his injuries were and he didn't seem like he needed to go to the hospital, but he looked terrible. Momma was at work and

Cookie was living with us at the time and was in charge. At thirteen years older than the youngest of us, she took her duty seriously. If Momma wasn't there, she had to act as if she was our mother.

So, when Jackson walked in looking like he did, she stopped him short, ready to get answers just like she knew Momma would have. "What on earth happened to you? Explain this."

"Some fools jumped me," he told her. Cookie flew into action; she pumped Jackson for details without cracking a smile. As soon as Momma got home from work, Cookie updated her on the situation in hushed tones. Momma came out into the living room where Cookie, Bronson, Daniel, Jackson, and I were waiting to see what she was going to do. I was stunned as I saw her sliding her gun into her pocket.

"Put your shoes on," she calmly told them. "You're gonna walk around there, while I drive the car. We'll see who is over at the park."

They did as they were told and filed out of the house. Jackson looked pale and nervous. Maybe he was starting to pick up on where this was headed. Then Momma took Jackson and Daniel aside, cocked her gun, and told them to go out back and grab their bat.

I heard none of that, the boys told me about it years later, but I was still surprised. Second-grade me didn't understand what was happening, but I knew it wasn't good.

They walked around the neighborhood a bit, this strange, slow-moving cluster, but they didn't find the guys who had roughed up my brother. So, Momma loaded them in the car, and set off to find where the boys lived. She rounded a bend and there was a house right there with a porch full of people. And on that porch was the mother of one of the thugs who had jumped on my brother.

Momma called her out from where she stood.

"Them little bastards jumped on my son," she said with purpose. "Where are the groups of young boys who were just around the corner?"

And the lady said, "They're not here," which was not what Momma wanted to hear. She was not a starter, my mom, but you could not be a wimp around her and she certainly would never be one herself. So, she pressed further.

"I'm not going to play with you," she told her. "I'm asking you, where are the boys who just jumped on my son?"

"And I told you, they're not here."

Jackson looked at our mother, waiting for a reaction, and

seeming maybe like he was hoping that this meant we were finished here. We weren't.

"Well," Momma said back real slowly, "I guess I'm here to tell you that you must be raising cowards, wherever they are. Because they jumped on my son, four against one, and with no warning. And my son is coming back around here to have a fair fight. Because that wasn't it. And my son and I, and my whole family are ready to wait until those boys who jumped him around the corner are back. When they are, my son is going to have that fair fight."

The porch mom did not see that twist coming. "Oh," she shot back apprehensively, "he wants to have a...fair fight?" I couldn't blame the woman for her confusion and reticence. Not a thing about this was normal. Who learns their son has been worked over by a bunch of dudes and then...demands an immediate rematch?

Momma told her, "Yeah, and he knows which one he wants. My son wants to have a fair fight with the one that hit him first."

I was in silence hearing the full details. My brother stared straight ahead. The porch mom, amazingly, considered this request and then rose from her seat. She nodded lightly to Momma and swung her screen door wide, then leaned into the house to holler, "Okay, come out."

Right, of course, her son was in there all along. He filed out to the porch, looking a little confused to be summoned. A minute later, the others showed up just in time! Four or five outright thugs came walking down the street in a group. As soon as they caught sight of Jackson, they took off running right toward him, probably intending to pick up where they left off.

"No," their mom told them. "He wants to fight one of you." Momma had pulled Jackson aside at this point and whispered that he had better give this boy a beating he would remember. And then the fighting started and somehow Jackson was giving it his level best, looking like he knew what he was doing. Here was my kind, goofy brother and he wasn't just holding his own, he was giving this boy a beating. Let me tell you, that boy is fast.

Then, without warning, one of the other boys moved forward like he was about to jump in the fight to maybe level the playing field because clearly Jackson was winning this thing. Momma was in motion before she even realized it. She hit one of the boys, who flew backward. Then she grabbed the other mother by her throat and said, "I will snap your neck if you don't tell them to back up."

Hearing this I think I muttered, "Oh, my God." Daniel, who would have been ten at the time, was standing next to her and he could see that this was getting out of hand. He didn't move, though. He told me years later that he had overheard Momma once tell our sister, "You don't run unless you see me fall." So, at that moment, he knew she expected him to stay put. The other boy backed up. And at some point, someone called the police.

When they arrived, Momma explained the situation as she saw it and the fact that she had dragged her son over to this house for a rematch. She was so pleasant with the cops, like this was a perfectly normal thing. Gone was the minutes-ago demeanor of a gun-toting woman who was threatening to snap a neck. Back were the silky tones of the woman who prayed over her sons and daughters every morning before they set a foot off her porch. "Lord Jesus, let your blood cover these children and protect them on their way to and from school. Please shield them from anyone going after them, from kidnappers, and from dogs."

Amazingly, the officers took my mom's side and they escorted the lot of us back around the corner after telling those hood-lums, "If I hear about y'all touching any one of these boys again, you're going to jail."

For Momma, this wasn't her being two-faced. It wasn't her being a woman of God on one hand and then abandoning it in the face of street violence. What I want to make you understand is what I realized on that day: the boldness she showed that day and the way that she in many ways always lived on the edge wasn't in conflict with her relationship with God. No, her boldness was actually a product of her relationship with God!

I'm not going to pretend that thinking of her that day doesn't still make me proud. I think of the story of David and Goliath in the Bible, where we learn that when you mess with God's children and then he strikes back with power, you're told not to be mad because you know that God's children are protected. So, if you come at them, you can't be shocked that there are consequences.

I believe that that's what my mom felt happened that day. That was her mindset. And that's what made her do it. When I look back on it now, it makes me want to be that for my children as well, for them to be able to come to me and say, "Mom, I have a problem," and know with absolute certainty that they can give that concern to me and it will be handled.

I probably wouldn't act exactly the same way she did, because, nowadays, people are a little bit crazier. But I can't guarantee you that. if my son came to me with a black eye, what I would do. Do I see myself calling the police right away? I don't know. Maybe I would run out the house, asking him to show me who did this. Or maybe I would be on the phone to one of my brothers, telling them to come over because we have something that needs to be handled together.

I've been in situations before, once I got older and I was in a relationship, where I didn't call the police, but instead called one of my brothers and said, "I need you to ride with me. There's a girl whom I need to talk to, and I need to do it tonight because I just need to tell her that she's never going to put her hands on my vehicle, and she's never going to disrespect me again in the club. And I need you with me." And my brother would say, "Okay, Sis, calm down. I'm on my way, and I'm just gonna be with you because I know you're just as crazy as I am!"

So, I'm not sure exactly what I'll do if that moment comes. But as a mother I want my children to know that Momma's boldness has been passed to me. And that means that they are also not to be messed with.

I worry that maybe I didn't get the full helping of the boldness, though. About a year ago my brother (Bronson) called me out for always trying to figure out what everyone is going to think before I make a move. I try to think it all through. "But remember that you're a leader," he rebuked. "People want to copy off you for a reason. So quit worrying about what people have to say. That's one thing that I wish you got more of from Momma because, if you remember, Tiyah, she never cared what anyone had to say. You just have to have a little bit more of that in you. Shut out what other people might think, because if you're able to shield that, man, you're going to be something else!"

And I was like, "Wow, you really hit that nail on the head."

That talk brought back some aspects of Momma that I hadn't thought about in a while. Yes, she handled her business. She knew how to put out a man who disrespected her and she knew how to keep her offspring safe. But I had sort of forgotten how she also seemed to be able to do pretty much anything else that needed doing.

I remember watching her unloading wooden two by fours from the car one day and lining them up on the lawn.

"What are you working on there, Ms. Smith?" some neighbors asked as they ambled by. Momma was building a fence, she announced, and I remember the skeptical faces the neighbors pulled when they heard that. "You don't know how to build a fence; you don't know how to read those plans."

In fact, she knew how to do both, or she taught herself how to anyway, because a few days later they came back by to see a nicely built fence and Momma acting like she'd had this talent her whole life. She hadn't been thinking about those neighbors or their concerns in the meantime. And she certainly hadn't been doubting herself.

There was another time when another set of neighbors walked by to see that Momma had taken all the seats out of her car. They were just sitting on the sidewalk right in front of our house. And they said, "Ms. Smith, what are you doing taking apart your car, there? What's wrong with your car?"

There wasn't a thing wrong with Momma's car. She was wanting to reupholster the seats in her car. She was a seamstress and could sew beautifully, so she knew that she could recover the seats of her car if she had them out. They thought she was certifiable. What kind of person disassembles the inside of their car when they have no background in auto mechanics?

"Oh, Ms. Smith, you need to put those seats right back in now and take that automobile down to the shop. That's not the kind of thing that you can do on your own, now."

Even we kids were kind of embarrassed by what she was doing. All of these people were coming to comment on the spectacle of the lady down the street who thinks she knows something about auto upholstery just because she can make dresses.

But Momma didn't listen that time either. The next few days were focused on reupholstering those seats in camel leather, embroidered with crosses. She was crafting a rolling testament to her love for God. In no time, those seats were back right where they belonged inside the car, and they looked amazing. Every neighbor had to come by and take a look and compliment Momma on her workmanship. But she had known all along that she could do it.

She used to tell us, "Listen, I can't tell you which friends of yours are going to end up crossing you one day. I'll leave that up to you to find out. But I'll tell you this, sometimes when you see that there's something you want to take on, but they don't have the dream or the vision to see why you want to, then they don't need to hear any more about it. It's okay to keep some things to yourself until you get it done. Because sometimes when people don't understand your motivation or your drive, they will come up against what you're trying to do and try to make you not do it. You don't need to listen; you don't need to tell them what you're planning to do. Just get it done. And then after, you can show them what you did."

And that was certainly true for her. Not to sound arrogant, but she really could do anything.

ALWAYS ON HER OWN

Momma's relationship with God made her bold enough to

live on the edge. But I think that her upbringing also made her believe she needed to be completely self-sufficient because she should plan to be on her own.

Momma grew up with one brother, my Uncle Sonny, in a devoutly religious single-parent home. Uncle Sonny knew his dad, but he was gone before Momma was born. She, however, never met her father. My grandmother, Dear, was their sole provider and caregiver from the beginning. She was also the person who taught my mom to love the church. Grandma was the very definition of saved and sanctified; she received the gift of knowing the presence of the Holy Ghost later in life, in her thirties, but her relationship with God was so strong, she went to church three, four times a week.

The religious structure that Momma got at home probably seemed to folks like the perfect fit for her. Really, she spent her childhood trying hard to be the ideal daughter for her devoted church lady mother. It wasn't always natural to her, but she would tell me that she was always, "trying to be pleasing in Dear's sight."

"My Momma didn't have anything to give me," she said, "but the word of God and a nice, warm house that I could come to if I needed to." My Momma was grateful for her upbringing and thus never went through a rebellious phase during childhood. Her brother, on the other hand, seemed ready to rebel from the start.

By the time Uncle Sonny was thirteen, he had had enough of the pious life and walked right out of my grandmother's house without looking back. He never returned to living with my grandma, and despite being barely in his teens, made his own way in the world from then on.

Momma loved her brother, but they could not have been more different. Even as adults, she played the role of the responsible, God-fearing sister when they were together while he never quite stopped rebelling against the values they had been raised on.

My earliest memories of Uncle Sonny took place when we still lived in Chicago. I remember him coming to visit and spending time with my brothers and me. He was playful and funny and a joy to be around. The four youngest of us, especially, looked forward to his visits; we lit up when he was around.

Uncle Sonny's personality was larger than life and so was his physical presence. While my grandmother was a tiny thing of about five-foot-nothing and Momma was five-foot-six, Uncle Sonny somehow clocked in at six-foot-two and some 300 pounds. He could talk his way into, and out of, almost anything. And oh, my God, was the man gifted at math! Give him any problem and he'd shoot the answer back at you. And that's just how he talked around us. He made it seem like he knew everything and we ate it right up. We kids loved to hear him talk, sitting cross-legged on the floor, looking up at him like he was a teacher in class.

Momma saw a very different side of her brother. His smarts and charm worked on her, but she also always knew that the next patch of Uncle Sonny-generated trouble was never far away. By the time I knew him, Uncle Sonny had grown into a first-rate con man. And it was her job to protect the family she built from the fallout. Uncle Sonny had spent some time in the military. He had married a beautiful woman and became a stepfather. Neither lasted long, though I'll never be sure if we got the true story about why either ended. It was always hard to tell where fact ended and fiction began with Uncle Sonny.

One recurring lie was that he had more children than Momma. "You may have given birth to twelve, Hattie, but I've still got you beat," he would tell her. I knew Uncle Sonny my whole life and never met a single cousin who came from him. That didn't stop him from resurrecting the claim every so often. When I was in my twenties he added on the kicker; Uncle Sonny would tell us that in addition to having more children than Momma, he also might not be done having them. He could father more children, too, if he liked. Okay, Uncle Sonny...

Before we left Chicago, Uncle Sonny did a stint in prison, so we didn't see him for a while. Then, one morning as she was leaving for work Momma told us that Uncle Sonny was due to be released and she was worried he was going to try to stay with us. She wasn't having it and forbade us from letting him in if he came by while she was not home.

"He's impossible to get rid of once you let him in and, besides, if you let him have the run of the house when I'm not here he's bound to steal something. Do not let him in this house. Do you understand me?"

You couldn't blame Momma for worrying. Uncle Sonny wasn't about to steal the little figurine off your nightstand. He might not even take your wallet. But if he found something that could take him far and that could let him do what he wanted to do in the streets, he might take it. He might respectfully think that he had the right to it. And cars? Cars were his favorite thing to take!

His scheme was one of the most audacious I've heard. Uncle Sonny would tell people that he was a mechanic and agree to work on their car. As soon as the keys hit his palm, though, Uncle Sonny would just skip town with their car. He didn't always steal the cars; sometimes Uncle Sonny would come back with a vehicle three weeks later and return it.

So, now Uncle Sonny was about to be a free man and Momma had put the fear of God in us about letting him come into the house. Fast-forward a few days, and we four youngest were home alone and heard knocking on the front door. We ran up front and saw Uncle Sonny's face framed in the diamond window cutout of the door. H was smiling and waving at us and we just repeated that we couldn't open the door to him and to each other. And Uncle Sonny just kept on knocking, looking right at us through that window.

"Open this door; it's cold out here," Uncle Sonny told us.

We made it about a half hour before we let that man in. When Momma came home from work, she walked in to find her jailbird brother on her couch, feet kicked up, having just fed her children a homemade dinner of chicken and fries. We were all laughing at one of his stories. And poor Momma was just baffled. This visit lasted a few weeks; Uncle Sonny was being respectful and cleaning up after himself. She thought maybe he had finally turned over that new leaf. Momma would come home and find him talking with us about how he had read the Bible front to back. Growing up with a mind like his, in a house like Grandma's, he could quote any scripture. If you brought a chapter to Uncle Sonny, he'd always correct you if you were wrong. So, you'd better know what you're talking about!

One evening Momma was talking to him about God in our living room and saying to Uncle Sonny that it was time he gave his life up to the Lord. He turned to Momma and asked, "And you're still working in the lounge, right?"

That was true; Momma was serving drinks, spinning records, and whatever else that was none of my business, at a local lounge.

"Well," she told him, "God is working on me, too." But she explained that Uncle Sonny needed to make it right with God, to work on his bad manners, taking the Lord's name in vain. And Uncle Sonny didn't like that. He stood up and interrupted her with, "You're not going to come in here talking to me about God."

That was it. Momma pushed him clean out the door and she told him she would have his things out on the lawn for him shortly. She wouldn't have him talking badly about God in her house. That was the last straw for a while. But it didn't last forever. Momma was a nurturer, and this was her brother. Sometime after we moved to Wisconsin, the visits started back up again.

THE GOOD DAUGHTER

Uncle Sonny's rebellion began at age thirteen and never really stopped. Momma never rebelled, but she still found her independence at the very same age. She would end up moving out of my grandmother's house at thirteen as well.

Momma had grown up with a boy named Lewis in the church; they had known each other since they were little. He played in the congregation's band, and by the time Momma was a teen the two thought they were in grown-up love. Lewis had a summer job, so he was what passed for a man of means at thirteen, meaning he was able to sweep her off her feet and take her away from Grandma's. With Lewis's stash of cash, the two ran off to Mississippi to visit some family and came back married! At fourteen, their little family got larger; Momma got pregnant with her first child and a second baby came soon after. With Cookie and Bryson to take care of, the couple stayed married for a few years, but around the age of seventeen, Momma became a divorcee.

Freed from her marriage for the first time Momma was both a woman and single. She had been a child when she married Lewis and now she was actually grown. She told me of that time in her life, that it was so much more fun to talk to men once she was an adult. Momma was enjoying dating and soon fell in love with a man named Joe. She was thrilled when she got pregnant again and overjoyed when she and Joe welcomed their daughter, Princess, into the world.

The new parents' happiness didn't last long; Momma soon lost her baby daughter to what was then called crib death, which we now know as sudden infant death syndrome. Princess was only three months old. The period that followed was likely Momma's first serious bout of depression. She locked herself away, refusing to get out of bed except to care for Cookie and Bryson. Gradually, she emerged from the darkness, but the loss changed her. She was no longer able to connect and it wasn't long before she and Joe went their separate ways. I didn't learn about the final tragedy of that era until years later: Joe was murdered one night on the streets of Chicago.

A marine on leave would be the next man to sweep Momma off her feet. She fell hard for Melvin and gave him a son. My brother Hardy would eventually follow in his dad's footsteps and join the Marine Corps. Momma once told me, in a whisper, that Hardy's father was the one man she remained crazy about to that day.

"But a woman took him from me," she said. "This someone came along and she had more than me. I was so proud that I was finally becoming a woman, but here she was already established. Compared to her, I didn't interest him anymore. I remember the heartbreak I felt after that," Momma told me.

With their romantic relationship over, Momma decided not to be angry at him. She tried to forge a friendship so that Hardy's dad would remain in his life. Still, she couldn't be in Chicago anymore, the site of her heartbreak. Momma packed up and moved to St. Louis where she had some cousins.

The Missouri years that came next weren't ones we heard about much, but all of us knew they hadn't been good ones for our mom. She met a man she hardly talked about, someone she quickly left when he became mentally unstable and abusive. Once again, Momma fled a city to escape some relationship drama. She retreated to Chicago, not even knowing she was pregnant at the time.

At the age of twenty-two, Momma found herself alone again, caring for three young ones, and surprised to be pregnant with baby number five. She told me this was a time of struggle, managing her life while still healing from her baby's death and the trauma of an abusive partner. She wasn't looking for another husband, just peace. As she settled back into the neighborhood and motherhood, she found companionship in a neighbor who was thirty years her senior. Stephen from around the way would just turn up on her stoop. They would pass the time, get to know each other, and eventually he just started trying to help her out. "Are you okay today, Hattie? You need anything? Can I help you with something?"

Momma told me Stephen would bring the kids food, buy all kinds of stuff for her, and just be there for her to talk to. Before she had even given birth to my brother Doeboy, their friendship had transitioned into something more. Ten months after Doeboy arrived, Momma and Stephen welcomed my sister, Precious.

I wonder what would have happened with Stephen if the timing had been different. Was he a good enough man, the right match, who could have been her true partner? If Momma hadn't still been healing from her baby's death and from the trauma of abusive relationships, would she have stayed once the honeymoon period ended? Would she have had the energy to put in the work once their fighting began? As it was, she just didn't have it in her to put up with Stephen as more and more arguments popped up. Momma told me that she just wasn't interested as she had once thought and so she couldn't stay to deal with it. Just like that. Stephen was out.

After Stephen, Momma started spending more time at church. Time and God were easing her pain and she was doing alright by herself. Her mother and her aunt soon introduced her to Elder Charles the First, and a nice friendship blossomed. They enjoyed spending time together and had many values in common. Soon, Elder Charles asked Momma for her hand in marriage and she agreed. The two ran off to get married and returned to find there would be far more than just the two of them in their new marriage.

Momma's mother and aunt started in her ear, right away, telling her not to mess this marriage up. Elder Charles the First was established. He was a man of means and I'm sure they meant well in pushing Momma to treat him well, keep him happy, and secure this new family. They wanted to make sure she was being a good wife to her new husband whom they thought was, "so good!" Elder Charles the First's family certainly agreed, and they were also all up in the newlyweds' business. His sister, in particular, was always around. She had never married and had many opinions about the newlyweds' life together.

While they were still settling into being husband and wife, Momma and Elder Charles the First learned they were pregnant with twins. Along came Elder Charles the Second and Ledosha, adding to the pressure that the new couple felt. Momma stuck it out for a few more years, but the families' involvement eventually became too much for them both. They parted but remained good friends. It's truly a testament to Momma that after that split she not only kept Elder Charles the First so close to her and her children but found a way to stay tight with his entire family. Down the line, Momma even asked Elder Charles the First's sister to be my godmother. Godmother, without any children of her own, was honored to be asked, and threw herself into the role. I couldn't have asked for a better godmother.

FINDING OUR FATHERS

As I was growing up, when Momma would tell me the stories of the men who came before Dee, the thing that struck me was how hard she had worked to keep each of our fathers in our lives if she could. She wasn't keeping these men close to the family for her. Momma never asked for child support or alimony from any of her husbands. Heck, I'm not sure how many of them helped with finances even during their marriages. She saw the value of fathers and what knowing ours would have for her life.

People judge Momma. It's one of the big things I worried about when I decided to write this book. They see a woman who couldn't make five different marriages work and someone who wasn't able to give any of her children a household that included their father. All I ask of those of you when you think about Momma is that you see the context, the color around her story. I'm not saying she was perfect. But look at the leap she made in one generation. Here is a woman who never set eyes on the man who provided one half of her DNA. And in a single generation she was able to give most of her children relationships with their dads.

The part that hits me right in the gut, though, and which might do the same to you if you think about it, is that she knew to respect the value of our fathers without ever having experienced it firsthand. She was a fatherless daughter who never stopped fighting to make sure the next generation knew what it was to be fathered. It's sort of beautiful, and also a little tragic.

I often marvel at how Momma created family that stretched across exes and DNA. We never said half-sister or brother. We didn't understand that language because all of Hattie Smith's children were one big family.

For us four youngest kids, that meant we got some extra fathers asking after us. My other brothers' and sisters' dads embraced us. They would stop by and be like, "Oh, my God, that's the baby!" when they saw me. (Whether I was ten, fifteen, or twenty I would forever be the baby of this family…)

Wherever we went within that larger family network we were welcomed. You could just feel the love. The dads followed my mom's lead; their attitude toward their children's half siblings was just, "That's your brother. That's your little sister." That's how they worked.

I've got to give my mom respect for that. It was all about how she carried herself after a breakup. Maybe she had complaints about her most recent ex. Maybe she had some steam to let off. But no one else could say a thing about our fathers. That went for all of us. The dads in our family were off-limits. She made sure that respect was always there.

"You don't disrespect your dad; he loves you, okay? Even though we had our thing, he's crazy about y'all."

Those are the talks she would have with each of us. Mom made a place where everybody belonged and was worthy of kindness. Sure, you could say I wasn't old enough to remember any of these breakups. That's true. But throughout my whole childhood I overheard her conversations with these men. These were guys who had done her wrong, whom she might have been really mad at during a certain moment. But that's not what she showed me.

I have so many memories of her walking into the house and finding my brother or sister on the phone with their dad. She would just put out her hand, waiting for them to pass her that receiver.

"Let me talk to him," she would say matter-of-factly. "Hey old man, how you doing?"

No matter which one of her exes was on the other end, that's how she got on the phone. She had made children with that man. He was the father of her children. So, they were in each other's lives. They were each other's people. She was never a bitter woman. She just never was.

"Oh, hey Hattie," they would say. "I'm doing this, and I just did that."

With each and every one of them, that's how their talks would go: no rushing to get off the line, no pretending to be interested just to keep the peace. And I never once heard, "You didn't send this. You didn't send that. You know what, I'm taking you to court." Words like those never passed her lips.

NO TIME TO WAIT

During my life so far, I've thought a lot about the pattern of my mother and men. As thankful as I am for the fathers she gave us, I never wanted to repeat her patterns. And then

I did. Until I didn't. And the thing that I always come to when I think about what was missing for her was that she didn't know how to just stop and wait. Momma's relationships always ended when she was betrayed or disappointed or let down. And sometimes those things are genuinely insurmountable. But sometimes they just take a minute. She didn't want to sit in that uncomfortable feeling. Momma needed to just keep moving. "Oh, you've let me down. Okay, well it's going to end then, so we might as well do it now. Let's make a clean break, keep things friendly, and get on to the next thing."

That's how I picture Momma's mind working. She didn't like the messy part, so she just started over, again and again and again.

I often wonder what it would have been like if she had her father present, same as I wonder that about myself. Momma always told me that her reason for having a lot of children was because she was lonely growing up. It was just her, her mother, and her brother. Then Uncle Sonny ran away and the two women were alone. The men in her life had abandoned her, and in some ways, she would spend the rest of her life having a hard time allowing herself to be vulnerable and love her husbands because she was looking for something in them that she never received from her father. She never even saw a picture of the man.

Spiritually, that's how she moved through life, through every single relationship, looking for something she was missing and thinking she was going to get it from these men. And so, Momma gave herself to them. She married them. She had their babies. She began to make a family for them. And then they did something that said the same thing her father's absence said. It said, "You're not enough." So, she couldn't sit with that. It was too familiar and too painful. So, she had to move on.

When I think back to the scene with the gang members and my brother, I believed it was all about Momma's bravery at the time. But now I know it was also about fear. My mother refused to live in fear of when her son would be jumped again. But she knew it would happen. So instead, she took the risk that he could be seriously hurt or killed that night, rather than wait for that day to come. That was the same move she made on her husbands. Once she knew they were going to hurt her, she couldn't wait for them to do it again. She needed to make it hurt now, so it could at least be over. The waiting wasn't for Momma.

CHAPTER 3

Taken Advantage

"When you begin to realize that your past does not necessarily dictate the outcome of your future, then you can release the hurt. It is impossible to inhale new air until you exhale the old."

—BISHOP T.D. JAKES

I've got some holes in my memory from the time between Dee moving out and us settling into our last house in Chicago. But I've got this vivid, warm memory from once we moved into that house.

I'm in the living room, playing on the floor with my youngest brother. The front door bangs shut and the two of us jump to our feet in surprise; we hadn't heard anyone pull up. When we see who it is, though, a small smile passes between us. We know what's coming next. Then, in a blink, my brother's smiling face fades quickly into a blur and I'm airborne.

The room whizzes past me as I gulp air from about five feet off the ground. I hear snippets of, "Hey there," and "Get over here," which let me know that the rest of the family has heard the arrival and started spilling into the living room from other parts of the house.

I can't concentrate on them, though. My focus is the secure feeling of my big brother's arms tight around me as he spins us. His heart is beating double time where I'm pressed against his chest, and I'm grinning so hard that I probably look like an idiot. But it's hard to care when I feel so much joy.

Today's not a special occasion. On any given weekend at our house the scene's pretty much the same. Sometimes I hear the car coming, and then I'm up and running toward my brother's arms before he comes in. We get a lot of these visits because, even though my oldest siblings are out and living on their own now, they can't stay away long.

After the spinning and the hugging and the hellos, everyone sits to catch up. I scramble into my brother's lap and check out the gifts that he and the other older siblings may have brought me. My older siblings spoil me and not just with presents. They're asking about my week. Is everyone treating me nicely? The unspoken part coming through loud and clear: "We've got your back, Tiyah. We're here to protect you."

Months later, when the Monster arrived and everything changed, it would be days like today that I missed like crazy.

NEW HOUSE, WHO DIS?

There was a tough year or so in there before we would land in that last Chicago house. During their separation and divorce, Dee and Momma had lost the home on Claremont that they had been proud to be able to have together. Momma was pretty mad about it. "That man cost me our home," she would tell me. For her to make even a passing negative remark about one of the dads meant it really hurt her to lose that home.

But Momma was also realistic. There wasn't much to be done other than find a new place for us kids who were still living at home. As I started work on this book, I realized I had almost blocked out what came next. Momma moved the four of us into a house that had been abandoned in the neighborhood. I used to talk about the vague memories I had of spending time in that backyard, as if it was just a playhouse we once had. That's how my mind had made sense of it, I guess. But it wasn't a playhouse. The homeowners had moved out, perhaps due to foreclosure, and we were illegally squatting while Momma got her feet back under her.

I'm not sure how long my three siblings and I spent in that abandoned property. Was it a couple weeks? Were we there a couple months? I just remember being happy when it came time to move into a home that was really ours.

Life was pretty good once we moved into our new house. I'm not saying that my siblings and I liked that my parents divorced. But we were together and happy, and the new way of living was okay.

We moved across Chicago to a new neighborhood and into a single-family house with an upstairs this time. The house was tucked next to an open field on a residential block, with a big backyard out behind, too.

The neighborhood felt quieter and more suburban than where we lived before, and it came with new schools and friends for all of us. And then there were the bike girls.

Three houses from ours, down the street, lived a couple of girls who would come by every day while I was playing in the yard. And oh, man, their bikes. They had these beautiful bikes; they were just so cute. They had those tassels on the handlebars and they were pretty colors. And, I didn't have that. But I wanted it. I wanted bikes like those badly.

My brother and I had wheels. We had brought scooters with us from the old house. They were little plastic scooters in bright colors, just three wheels, and you could maybe get a blue one or a purple one. But that was about all the style there was to them. No glittery tassels, no pastel pinks, or pleasing shades. And they tore up easily if you were too heavy and got on it.

But I loved watching these new girls go past. They had little horns up at the front of those bikes, tassels streaming, as they laughed and pedaled by. And I dreamed of having one.

So, there I was, just getting used to my new space, being a kid. Starting to learn that there might be some material things out there that other kids had that we didn't, that I was maybe going to covet and want and wish for in a new kind of way. That concept of our poverty was starting to poke in. But I wasn't yet too bothered by it.

John Wayne Gacy changed that...

KILLER CLOWNS AND UNDERPASSES

I mean, he didn't show up at our house or anything. But *the stories* about John Wayne Gacy did start showing up. Around this time, I remember that people all around us started talking about the kidnapping clown who was terrorizing Chicago.

Today, it's years later and we all have Google. So, it's easy for me to do a quick search and know that these timelines do not match up. Gacy was already in prison by the time I was in elementary school. He had been tried for his crimes and was safely locked away. So, I can't tell you what made him become a common topic of conversation all over again for the parents around me. Maybe there was news coverage of his incarceration or something else happened to throw his name back into the headlines. Whatever it was that got the adults talking, though, I can assure you this: they sure didn't make it clear to my little ears that the monster clown was already put away. None of us kids picked up on that part of the story. So, for us, this was a real and present danger.

Then my mom started telling us to attach ourselves to other kids in the neighborhood. That scared me. For the first time it seemed like she thought that maybe just my brothers and I weren't enough of a pack on our own.

"When you walk, if you see other neighborhood kids walking, you try and get in with that crowd; don't be too far behind that crowd," she started telling us.

There was this bridge, a viaduct we called it, that we had to walk under to make it to the school. It was the subway up top, and underneath wasn't a road; cars didn't drive on the underneath part. It was just a dirt area where you could walk, so there often wasn't anyone around down there except for whoever you were walking with.

Once my mom had showed us her hand, letting us know she

was nervous about someone grabbing us kids and throwing us into a van, that part of the walk in particular got a whole lot scarier! As far as we knew, the killer clown we heard them all muttering about was still on the loose and this might be his best spot to snatch us.

That stretch under the viaduct was probably close to half a mile away, and if you try to picture it you can imagine why it felt kind of shady under there. No one was around. It was far enough from home that whatever neighbors might have been closest—not that there were any nearby—don't know you from Adam. Someone could pull right up under that bridge and just snatch us up and take us off, with no one being the wiser.

That kind of thing had just never occurred to me until that fall after we moved. I had never even known that this was something that happened. But once my eyes were opened to the idea, I couldn't unlearn it.

I was seven that year, and the others were nine, eleven, and thirteen. Some of the kids who we would be walking with thought they were pretty funny, even though looking back I'm sure they were just as terrified as I was. And they would sometimes play the worst game ever: "Oh, I see a van!"

The rest of us would take off running! We would seriously be ready to kill each other just to get out of there, running over each other and trying to climb up on the sides of that bridge to get out from under the area and away from the van that we just knew had a killer clown in it. We just knew that today was the day that he had come for us, and we were not going out like that.

HELLO, MONSTER

That snapshot's funny, because while John Wayne Gacy was a genuinely terrifying human, he wasn't coming for my brothers and me. By 1994 he had been executed by the state. What's not funny is that there was another real-life-monster out there that *it would have been* reasonable for me to worry about. This one was also true to life and terrible, but unlike Gacy, he was actually about to darken our doorstep. I just had no idea he was coming.

Dee had been out of our house for about a year and a half when Momma first started bringing Tracey around. She was still working at that lounge that had caused such a rift between her and Uncle Sonny. Owned by one of her cousins, the venue was a restaurant on one side, and on the other side a bar and dance floor. Tracey knew one of her cousins, so he came around the lounge often to mingle.

Tracey was about twenty-six, well outside Momma's normal dating pool, and she wasn't even considering him as anything but a friend. As soon as they met, I think Momma could sense that he needed rescuing. That was a talent of hers: seeing who the walking wounded were. She would bring them home, feed them, include them in the love of our family, and nurse them back to spiritual and emotional health. That's who Tracey was to her at first, someone whom God had called her to help. They had spent time talking and Tracey had shared snippets with her of his very troubled upbringing. He claimed that his father had accepted money from a neighbor in exchange for taking sexual liberties with his underage son. Tracey told her he was raped repeatedly while his father profited off this arrangement with the man down the street. Momma heard this story and wanted to save this young man whom nobody had cared to save and protect as a child.

These were the stories Tracey was telling my mom when he would come over and have dinner with us. Sitting around he always made everybody laugh. Tracey was so funny that he seemed to fit in with our collective sense of humor right away. My sister used to be dying laughing, trying to eat her dinner in between guffaws. He set the whole family at ease from the beginning, and even though Momma had taken him on as a project, they started spending more and more time together and eventually began dating. Soon Tracey started spending some nights at our house, something that hadn't really happened before. But I'm not sure any of us thought anything of it. This was such a nice guy; he didn't look like a mess. He was fifteen or so years younger than my mom, but he took care of himself, dressed nicely, and just fit in well.

THAT NIGHT

Tracey wasn't shy or quiet; he was very open. So, as he started spending more and more nights at the house, it seemed pretty natural. I think we had lived in the new home about six months before he moved in officially. He bunked in Momma's room, of course, which was up on the second floor. My sister had a room upstairs, and there was a third room on the second level that my brothers shared. I still didn't quite have a room of my own, so some nights I spent upstairs with my sister, and others I slept on the couch downstairs. It was on one of the couch nights that Tracey turned into the Monster.

On that night I fell asleep cuddled on the couch next to one of my brothers, but at some point, he woke up, realized how late it was, and trudged upstairs to his own bed. So, when I woke up on the couch with someone next to me, I didn't realize at first that it was Tracey. As he came into focus, I saw that he was holding a finger over his mouth, telling me to keep quiet. My seven-year-old brain, still a bit sleep addled, wasn't processing the weirdness of it, but now it's all I can think of, how far gone he must have been to approach me like this.

See, the angle of the stairs up to the second floor meant that if you were upstairs, the second you put a foot onto the top step the whole sofa was in full view. Tracey should have known, living in this house, that this meant if Momma hit the top stair, she would have seen everything that was about to happen. There would have been no time to cover anything up. There wouldn't have been time to fix anything.

Because of the way I was hanging off the couch, I could look up over my head and see the stairs. I was staring at them and waiting. When I looked back to where Tracey was, I realized now that he wasn't beside me on the couch, but on his knees in front of me. As I looked at him, he reached forward and pulled my body up, to where my legs were off the couch, but my back was still on. And he started pulling down my underwear. I was still looking at him, and chills started to run over me. I was confused. I didn't know what was going on.

But my eyes kept feeling pulled back to looking up at those stairs. My brain wasn't sure what was happening, but it was as if my eyes already knew to call for help. What I remember so clearly from being there was continuing to slide my eyes over to the top of those stairs, just waiting and hoping that somebody else who lived in this house would appear at the top step and help me figure out what's going on. There are a lot of people in the house at this point, right? My three brothers are up there. My sister had stayed at her boyfriend's house that night, but Momma was right up there, asleep in her room, too. Surely someone would show up in a minute.

Years later, when I finally talked about what happened with Momma, she said that was the most sickening part. That the Monster climbed out of bed with a woman to go mess with a little girl. He was so sick that he watched, he waited, and then he preyed on me as soon as he saw his chance.

When my eyes next went back to Tracey, I saw that he now had this little smirk going, like we were sharing a joke, like maybe he was about to tickle me or something. And I remember looking in his face, and realizing it was getting closer to me. He had finished pulling down my underwear and had pulled himself out of his. The move forward had allowed him to line his genitals up with mine, and I felt him rubbing on the outside of my vagina. It's then that I realized I was completely frozen. I had been since I woke up to him telling me to be quiet, but it was only now, when I would have liked to have moved far away from what was happening to my body, that I realized fear had me paralyzed.

While I lay there, half on and half off the couch, still staring at his face, he continued to move, rubbing himself up and down, up and down on the outside of my vagina. And then we heard a noise.

We heard a noise from upstairs and he stopped immediately. It was as if he had snapped out of something and was thrown into motion. He shoved himself back into his underwear. He tugged my underwear up and put it right. As he pulled up my underwear, he kind of pushed my legs back onto the couch and made a move to get up. Then he stopped and put that same finger over his mouth again, this time looking up at the stairs pointedly. Then the Monster disappeared.

I stayed right where I was. I lay down there on that couch by myself. Only a few moments had passed since I had been asleep, but they had changed everything. I felt hot shame crawling all over my face and my body and I didn't even know why. The instant he was gone I felt guilty. And then isolated. I stayed down there alone the whole rest of the night, eyes on the stairs. I don't think I shut them until morning. But I couldn't let myself go upstairs to my family, either. All of a sudden, there seemed to be a huge gulch separating us. I was on my own.

At some point I must have given in to sleep because the next thing I knew I was waking up to the sun shining in through the windows in our living room. My mom had hung mirrors on the wall that connected to one another to form a line of diamond shapes. The sun was hitting those mirrors and making diamond patterns on the walls. And I remember coming to, still on that couch, still alone in that living room, and staring at those sun diamonds with my mind entirely blank.

Eventually, I stood and went upstairs, and that's when I remembered my underwear. They were soaked. I took them off and worried why they were so wet. I stared at them in my hand and wondered: was it from him or from me? I didn't know what my question even meant. And I didn't know what to do with my ruined underwear.

NOTHING TO SEE HERE

For his part, Tracey went on with life as we knew it. He acted as if nothing had happened. That day, and the next day, and next week, and the next month were all totally average. Everything was normal. My brothers didn't know that anything had happened. Momma didn't know that anything had happened. But in my head, I knew that something giant had changed. And I felt like I was now different too, somewhere deep down.

It was a few months later that I remember Momma and Tracey starting to bump heads a little bit. They started having disagreements because she started noticing things coming up missing. My uncle had been to visit recently, so, of course, he was the first suspect. But when Momma questioned Uncle Sonny he swore up and down that it wasn't his work this time. Now that she had involved him, though, Uncle Sonny seemed to want to help her get to the bottom of it. And one night they must have found something that proved Tracey was the one stealing from us, because Momma and Uncle Sonny just decided he needed to be put out of the house.

I think Momma had found out that Tracey was cheating and

doing some other things that she didn't like, but it just put the icing on the cake. As she confronted him about the stealing, they got into an altercation and Momma didn't like how close he came to putting his hands on her, and she just went at him. My uncle joined in, and the two of them essentially carried him right onto the street. That was the big breakup.

I was relieved that Tracey was gone, but as Momma realized that he had also been stealing money from her she started worrying about upcoming bills. During the next couple months, she struggled financially, and it was the final blow to living in Chicago. We had been paying between $600 and $800 a month in rent for the properties we had lived in in Illinois, and she said we could get a house for half that if we were willing to move to Wisconsin. Momma started to talk about what it would be like to be able to get ahead financially instead of just covering our bills. She was ready to make a life for herself and her family in a way that might be easier to sustain. The decision ended up being an easy one: the Smith family was moving to Milwaukee.

Hitting the road sounded good. I was feeling so uncomfortable in my skin that a change of scenery was welcome. I was presently worrying my days away, convinced that my brothers could see right through me, to the shame and filth I was now carrying inside me. A move would bring a distraction as I learned how to hold part of me secret from the people with whom I had always shared my whole self. And the best part of the move was the chance to put miles and miles between me and the Monster. I could be sure that I would never see his terrible smirk again.

CHAPTER 4

Starting Over and Going Backward

"Here's the bottom line with shame: the less you talk about it, the more you got it. Shame needs three things to grow exponentially in our lives: secrecy, silence, and judgment."

—DR. BRENÉ BROWN

Milwaukee would end up being special to me for a lot of reasons, but the first and biggest milestone that it held for a seven-year-old Atiyah was a room of my own. For the first time in my whole life, I had a bed that was reserved every night for only me, in a room where only I slept. It was a monumental change. Momma helped me choose all of the colors for my new room and let me make it as girly as I wanted. We bought a beautiful new comforter for my bed, and then Momma sewed flouncy, ruffled pillowcases to match it all.

The boys and I started right into school in our new neighborhood, and it felt seamless. I liked my teachers, my classmates, and my school. This new city was greener, there was more space everywhere, and it held the promise of leaving Chicago behind and never again having to think of what happened on that couch. I threw myself into our new life and started to believe that maybe moving on really could be this easy.

We had been in Milwaukee for half a year when I came home to find the Monster in my living room. As soon as I saw him, my whole heart sunk into my stomach. I don't think I hated him. I didn't know to hate him. A feeling of dread came over me as soon as I saw him somehow plucked from my nightmares and deposited into this clean, fresh, new life we had been starting to build. I did not care for this person being in my home. I walked out of the living room, went upstairs, and sat on my bed. I sat there for hours, thinking, "When are you going to do that again?"

I thought this was all behind me. But somehow, we had left a trail clear enough for this person to follow. And now he was here, a living reminder not just of what had been done to me, but of what could be done again. At any time.

Tracey was sick. There was something physically wrong with him, and it must have been really bad, because he looked terrible. It had only been a few months since we had seen him last, but the change was drastic. He had lost so much weight. He was drawn and pale. When I came back downstairs and rejoined the family, I only caught little snippets of their conversation because my mind was spinning. But it seemed from what I was hearing and the way they were interacting, that Momma and Tracey weren't back together. They weren't going to be dating. She needed to help him, though. There was no one else. And he was clearly in immediate need of being nursed back to health. Momma would move him in, just for a while, to make that happen. She wasn't forgiving him; she was instead doing her Christian duty. When he was back on his feet, he could get a place of his own and we could all move on.

It turned out, Momma wasn't going to move Tracey into our home upstairs with us. She worked out a deal whereby he could stay downstairs on our landlord's couch. I was told that chicken pox was the dreaded disease that Tracey was up against. So, Momma made soup, and took care of him. They talked and caught up, and he apologized for the stealing and dishonesty that had caused their breakup. It had been the drugs, you see, that made him act so deplorably. He was done with all that. Tracey wanted drugs out of his life for good. He wanted Momma's help to achieve that goal. Could she help him get into counseling and kick this habit once and for all?

Tracey was doing well living downstairs with our landlord, Lee, who had quickly become an honorary member of the Smith family. At seventy years old, Lee was still a man who could hold his own. We had been there less than a year, but in that time he and Momma had become good friends. We called them Beauty and the Beast because Momma was this lovely lady and Lee was this giant strong man with a big, gray beard and messed-up teeth. We were lucky to have found Lee because he looked out for us all. He owned his house and his car and had a good job. The young guys in the neighborhood respected him, and that gave us all a level of protection. One night, he and Momma were out listening to some music and a guy came up to talk to her and wouldn't take no for an answer. Lee punched the young guy so hard he flew across the room. He wasn't one to let Ms. Hattie be disrespected.

So, even though Tracey was back, I felt somewhat at ease knowing he was under Lee's watchful eye. We were living on separate floors and separate units, and if there really was something rotten about Tracey, surely kind, tough Lee would notice and keep me safe.

But a few months later, we got terrible news. Lee had suffered a heart attack on the job. He wasn't expected to make it. We lost our friend Lee and were all devastated. After his funeral we learned that Lee's daughter had inherited his properties and planned to sell them all. It was time to move again. It was never a conversation, but as the move was planned, Tracey was simply part of it. He was going from sick friend couch surfing downstairs, to member of the family. And I was powerless to do anything about it.

Momma found us a great new place on Center 26th Street, the block where we would live for the next fourteen years. This move was going to bring so many good things into our lives. The friends I would make on 26th Street remain among my best, and it's also where I would meet my first child's father. Tracey was more than ready to help with the move, no longer looking sick, having put back on some of the weight he had lost. He approached Momma and asked for another chance with her, and by the time we moved across town they were back together.

As summer started our family said goodbye to Lee's duplex and hello to a little red-and-white house of our own. The neighborhood was a step up from where we had been on the East Side of Milwaukee. It was busy and lively, and presented as tidy and clean. We didn't yet know that it had a busy drug scene, just that there were plenty of non-trafficking neighbors who generously welcomed us all to the neighborhood.

On any given day in our new neighborhood, I couldn't wait to get outside. On our street you would hear the birds chirping, music coming from a car down the block, and kids playing happily together. The next day you might hear the birds chirping, music playing from a car down the block, and a screaming fight in the middle of the street with the whole neighborhood trying to break it up or cheer it on…depending on who was involved. Either way, it kept us entertained!

As September crept in, Tracey was once again a fixture in our home, and Momma was getting us ready to blend into our new surroundings. My younger brother and I were starting at Clark Street Elementary, and the older two were entering the middle school. Momma spent the weeks leading up to the start of school reminding us to go up to our new classmates and introduce ourselves. She told us to find the groups of kids congregating and just work our way in. Some days Tracey would walk me to school, letting people think that I was his daughter. Then he got bolder, telling people we were his kids. Inside my head I was screaming, "No, no, no! I am not your daughter!" But with every day that went by with him acting normal and not trying anything with me again, I thought it was possible that nothing had ever happened in the first place. Maybe I had dreamed it all.

Momma got a new job and wasn't around as much, so she told my brothers it was their job to keep an eye on me while she was gone. This gave me some newfound freedom, which I used to go explore our neighborhood. Here, everyone was still trying to play tough. But you didn't have to worry about the colors you wore outside. I was a third grader, but in some ways, I felt like I was able to play around in my neighborhood as a kid for the first time. Of course, Momma's new job also meant more time alone with Tracey.

The layout of the new house put all three bedrooms on the second floor. My room, a huge room for Momma and Tracey, and a narrow room with bunks for the boys. I would get scared in my own room by myself, I was still getting used to having my own space, so I spent a lot of time with Momma in her room. Once she started the new job, I just kept up that habit. One day, my brother and I were lying on Momma's big bed watching cartoons, then he left to go outside. He had been gone a few minutes when I heard the door open.

Tracey was standing there in the doorway, and he started talking to me in this weird voice that he used to do that was supposed to be an impersonation of Dracula. He stepped into the room, and I immediately started looking beyond him, scouting both for my escape plan, and for any sign that we weren't alone together on this floor. In that house, if you looked out the door from Momma's room, you could see all the way down the long hall, past my brothers' room, to the steps. My mind started calculating again that as soon as someone reached the top of the stairs in this house, they could see what was going on atop the bed in Momma's room.

Tracey stopped talking in his vampire voice and started tickling me, making me laugh, until I was out of breath from the combination of wriggling and giggling. And I was starting to relax and think that maybe he had just come in here as his normal self, and I really didn't need to worry so much. And then he said to me, "Did you tell anyone? Because you know if you do, you're going to get in trouble." I was shocked. All of a sudden, the Monster was back, and sitting right on the bed with me. He pounced forward and pushed me back, then started kissing me, on my lips, on my neck. I didn't move. I couldn't believe this was happening again. As he kissed me on my stomach, he pulled down my underwear and kissed me on my legs. At some point he had taken himself out of his underwear because he was once again pressed against the outside of my vagina, rubbing himself all over me. I heard a noise, and I thought in that moment that it must be God stepping in because that couldn't be a coincidence. The same moment as when we were in Chicago, a noise stopped him, and now it was saving me again.

This time, Tracey wasn't done. He told me, "Stay right there, I'll be back," in the vampire voice and then walked into the hallway. I immediately started pulling back on my clothes, got off the bed and went into my room. Five minutes later one of my brothers came up and asked me to come outside with him, and it was over.

The next morning, he was back to walking me to school again, acting like I was his daughter. And I was back to spiraling inside of my head. It had been almost a year and a half since he had first assaulted me, and I had sort of let myself believe that it wasn't real. Now I had this fresh new hell to play over and over again in my head, plus I knew for sure that my first memory was as real as I had first feared. It got so loud inside my head.

"Oh, my God? What did I just do? Should I tell someone?

How much trouble will I be in that I didn't tell the first time? Is it my fault that it happened again? When will it happen next?"

A few months later, I at least got an answer to that last question. It wasn't going to happen again. Tracey had started stealing again, and Momma was done with his ways. She had put him out again, and all I could hope was that this time it would stick.

During that fourth-grade year I came very close to disclosing to one of my teachers. She was a wonderful woman and years later I ended up caring for her mom in a nursing home that I worked in. One day she asked me if I was okay. I wasn't, of course, and it felt for a second like this teacher could see through me. Could she tell that I was a mess inside? I started sobbing, just burst into uncontrollable tears and she told me, "You know, if somebody does something to you, you can talk to me. So, why are you crying? Can you tell me what's wrong?"

Ultimately, I didn't tell her. It just wouldn't come out. I sat there and cried and cried until she called Momma. When I got home, I was scared out of my mind. I didn't know if my teacher would have told her what she clearly suspected. Momma questioned me, asking what was wrong, reminding me that no one was allowed to mess with me, and saying that I could tell her whatever was upsetting me. I was so mad at myself for being weak, for almost showing what I had going on inside. And I was so relieved that my secret wasn't out.

I had a new friend by then, Porsha. When I was eight years old, I told her my secret. That's how we sealed our new friendship, by sharing a deep secret. When I described to Porsha what had happened to me, she ended up crying. And then she shared secrets of her own that she had never told anyone but me. We promised to keep these things between the two of us forever. So, at eight years old, this is the pact that I had with my new friend. I had disclosed my abuse to her alone and asked her to hold my burden.

CHAPTER 5

Hood Life

"The more you praise and celebrate your life, the more there is in life to celebrate."

—OPRAH WINFREY

We loved our new house; it was a definite step up from our last home. And the neighborhood was a big improvement from Chicago. I want you to understand that my Momma ran a clean house. And she raised clean children. But when we were living in Chicago, we had been in a place overrun with cockroaches and rats. When I tell you that these rats were huge, I know you're not going to picture them as big as they were because it's so hard to believe that we lived with these monstrosities walking among us. Let me put it this way: they were big enough that they didn't just fight back when you tried to get rid of them; they were aggressive. That's right. These rats chased us as children. I don't know if they thought of us as prey, or if they simply looked at us as playthings. And I was not trying to find out. I spent much of my life before we moved to Milwaukee planning how I would stay safe from those giant, angry rodents.

I remember one particular night when one of my older brothers was supposed to be watching Bronson and me, but he fell asleep on the sofa. I needed to go to the bathroom, but to do so I would have had to walk through the kitchen, and it was already dark out. That mattered, because at our house, as soon as the sun went down, the rats came out. I needed someone to walk me to the bathroom so that I didn't have to brave the rat-infested kitchen on my own. Bronson and I tried to wake up our so-called babysitter, to no avail. So, my sweet brother, only two years older than me and probably no less scared, said he would help me out.

We grasped hands and sprinted through the kitchen to the bathroom. I peed, and then we prepared to open the door. This second leg was the tricky part. On the first leg, when you were making your way through the kitchen toward the bathroom, you had the element of surprise on your side. The rats didn't know you were awake and coming their way. But now, they knew we were in here. No doubt they were waiting for us to come out. And, because they were bizarrely smart, they knew we wouldn't be in there all night. We would need to come back out at some point, and that's when they planned to get us. So, Bronson and I got ready to run. We clasped hands, swung the door open, and sprinted toward the living room as a team. We dove toward the sofa, toppling in a pile, panting and laughing. Just seconds after we made the jump, we heard a loud thud and felt the sofa shake. We looked down to see one of the rats peering up at us with his beady, little eyes. The thing was so bent on catching us that it ran right into the sofa. And the sofa shook when it did. I never did learn what it was those rats wanted with us, but the idea haunts me to this day...

This was by no means the only time that a rat chased us. Bronson would say they looked like horses coming toward us, galloping, weight on the back, then weight on the front. And that wasn't the only way they tortured us. There were times when the rodent problem got even worse and we found ourselves worried about getting nibbled while we slept. It happened to Momma's finger! I challenge you to fall asleep easily ever again once you've had the genuine worry that you would be awoken by a rodent nibbling on your toe.

You can bet that my brothers and I were working overtime to score sleepover invites at houses without problems like ours! Not that we were the only household dealing with these horse-rats! Chicago was known for their out-of-control rodents back then, and the problem apparently hasn't gone away. Last year, my brother who now lives in Virginia sent us a video from a trip he took back to Chicago to show us how crazy these rats still are. The video caught three big rats on camera, just roaming a neighborhood. Do a quick search online and you'll turn up hundreds of stories like this. But then again, you might not want to. Chicago rats are something you just can't un-see…

SHAKE IT OFF

Now that we were living in a rat-free house and Tracey had finally retreated for good, the two scariest things that had ever been inside my home were gone. That was no small blessing. But in Milwaukee we did learn that cockroaches offered a whole different kind of potential death: death by humiliation.

The rats in Chicago were only a problem at night. But now we had cockroaches with us all the time. No matter how sealed up all our food was and how crumb-free every surface and floor stayed, the roaches were permanent residents in Milwaukee. At first, they were more disgusting than scary because even though they were fast I knew I could always beat them in a fight. Still, we all hated when it was our night to do the dishes because you would always find yourself battling a sink full of roaches who thought the food waste you were trying to wash off would make a wonderful meal for themselves and their whole roach family.

The real damage that roaches could do, though, came when it was time to leave for school in the morning. We kids lived in fear of taking off our coat in homeroom and having a roach fall out of our hood or taking out a book from our backpack during math class only to have a roach be crawling atop it. These were totally reasonable fears, and despite how unavoidable roaches really were in our neighborhood, it's unlikely that we would have been able to live a moment like that down.

So, we had a ritual in the morning to prevent this potential embarrassment. Each day we would shake out our coats, and empty out our backpacks completely, just before heading out. We would shake, shake, shake, each item that needed to be added back into our backpack, to ensure that no stowaways remained.

My other ritual in Milwaukee was designed to keep mice away from me. Right, so our new home wasn't 100 percent rodent-free! We had really just upgraded to a kinder, gentler rodent. Milwaukee mice are scared of you, unlike Chicago rats. So, if they know you're coming, they're going to run. That's how we learned to live with the new roommates. My ritual became that every morning, before heading down to breakfast, I would have to throw stuff down the stairs ahead of me. That was the signal to the mice that I was coming, so they wouldn't run across my path. I knew they weren't going to hurt me. But seeing a mouse scurry past me was a terrible way to start the day. If I did, I would feel a full chill all over my body, and then I would have to shake it off and pretend that nothing just happened in order to get my head right for school—when a whole mouse just ran across my floor! Then, when I got to the kitchen, I would throw a shoe into the pantry in forewarning that I was coming there next.

I know these stories are funny, but part of you is probably also horrified at the conditions we were living in. I'll be honest, though, I wouldn't trade them. What I learned, as I walked through these scary, gross, and sometimes awkward situations with my siblings was that you can find joy in the midst of the most difficult circumstances. Families who pull each other through difficult circumstances and who can laugh when things are ridiculously difficult, stay together. And sometimes those truly are the best laughs you can get. The poverty we grew up in at times was crushing. As hard as Momma tried, there were nights when we went to sleep with empty bellies. And there were months when an unpaid electricity bill meant everything had to be plugged in via an extension cord that the neighbors were nice enough to run to our house. But it was never enough to kill our gratitude at having each other and our home.

I also counted on my siblings to help me deal with Momma. As amazing as she was, it was sometimes so hard to be her kid. See, when my mom was flush with food stamps at the start of the month, Momma would feed everyone. If a kid looked like they needed a good meal, a good talk, or even a firm hand, they were welcome at our table. Our friends, and even some neighborhood kids we didn't play with, all knew that if Ms. Smith had it, you were welcome to it.

Of course, that also meant we ran through our resources a lot faster than we might have had we not been saving the block from hunger during the first half of every month. Now, stores in our area gave credit to families, but even that could run out. So, even though Momma always worked and we had food stamps and store credit to lean on, toward the end of the month we were always stretched or out entirely. The end of the month was when you would find my siblings and me doing a full-court press to get dinner invitations at other houses. We also had a little friend who would loan my mom money to cover expenses. This was a boy of only ten or eleven, but he was stepping in! He had saved up all of his birthday money over the years, and because he loved Momma, he would just offer her loans. If he saw her struggling, he would just pop up with the $100 she needed, knowing that she always paid him back.

When Momma and Precious started working at a bus company, she cooked up a way to feed some neighborhood kids spiritually too. She asked her bosses if she could keep the bus with her over the weekends and use it to bring kids from the block to church. Momma would pack that bus with bodies every weekend and deliver a neighborhood's worth of young people to services. I was singing in the choir and enjoyed it all.

A POSITIVE TEST

Not all of my siblings had moved with us to Milwaukee and

I missed every one of them who hadn't dearly! So, summer became my time to head back to Chicago and see them. I would go visit for Christmas break too, but summer was the big visit. It became this long, magical time to spend with my oldest siblings and other family members.

After a few years, it also became a time when I started to learn some independence. We moved to Milwaukee when I was seven, and at first every visit I took to Chicago I went with Momma. But by the time my eleventh summer came around, though, I was old enough to go visit for a long stretch on my own. That was the very first summer I was allowed to catch the Greyhound bus by myself from Milwaukee. I rode the whole way on my own, just grown as I could be. I had very specific instructions about what to do when I got off in Chicago. My sister LaDosha was planning to meet me at the bus station on that end and had told me I was not to talk to a single person before she got there, and not to wander off. I was supposed to head straight to the pay phone, call her, and then sit on the bench right there and wait.

I did as I was told, sure. But that didn't mean I couldn't use my solo trips to start getting comfortable with being alone in the city. I would place my call as instructed, then I would head to the vending machine and get a soda and chips, or I would buy a hot dog. I would get back to my bench and people watch while I waited.

Once my sister collected me, it was all family, all the time. I had my siblings, my grandmother, and my extended family all around me.

One of my first stops would be to see my godmother. Elder Charles was one of my brothers who had stayed behind, and his auntie on his father's side was my godmother. She was probably sixty-five already by then, and I adored her. Godmother took me to church retreats every summer and made it her mission to teach me how to act like a lady. Maybe it was strange for a girl my age, but I couldn't get enough of spending time with Godmother, my grandmother, and their contemporaries. I poured out commodes and helped my grandmother and aunt wash up while they talked to me about stories from their day or dished out some truly excellent advice. It was in those summers that I started to realize my love of caring for the elderly. I had no idea what that would mean for me yet. But it was the first sign of what eventually would become my calling.

My grandmother lived in a high-rise apartment building just off the freeway for seniors. It was an independent-living facility, and she and her sister stayed there together, next door to each other. I would spend the night and my grandmother would have me help her around the house. I would put little things back in the refrigerator so she wouldn't have to work so hard, tidy up, and help her to get ready for bed. And then she would ask me to go next door to help her sister, who used a walker, to get ready for bed.

I was young, but it was clear to me they could both use a little support. This was a complex for seniors, but there was no one on-site who ran the building to help coordinate cleaning or in-home tasks. If you went down to the first floor, there was someone there who would help you out with making a phone call, and they were pretty nice. And there were vans that would come take you to church on the weekends and bible study during the week. If you wanted a caregiver to come help you with washing your clothes, cleaning up, or anything else, however, you had to locate, hire, and bring in an outsourced caregiver. And that's not always an easy thing to do. I think my brain stored that, and from that early time I was always thinking about how a living situation for women their age might have been better and done more.

When we drove into Chicago from Milwaukee, spotting that big, brown building from the highway is how I would know we were getting into the city: seeing White Sox Stadium and Grandma's building. Her apartment was a two-block walk to the stadium, so when fireworks went off, we could see them from her unit. Now that I have kids of my own, they know to look for that brown building, too; it tells them that the long drive's almost over. For me, it still tells me I'm back. It's that feeling of home that completes me.

That summer of my first solo Greyhound trip, home was kind of in two places for me. I still had my heart in Chicago, but I was also beginning to put down roots in Milwaukee. I returned from my trip, though, to a house in crisis. While I was away, Momma had gone to see her doctor because she hadn't been feeling quite right. He ran a whole battery of tests, then assured her they would get to the bottom of it. Then Momma got the call that we all dread. She had an issue with her blood that was likely to prove fatal. It was something she had caught from Tracey.

I wasn't there when Momma first found out. She was calm by the time I got back from Chicago. And it would be a long time before she filled me in on her diagnosis. But later I heard from my brothers that she had tried to kill Tracey when she first got diagnosed. They told me she spent a whole day driving around to the spots where he used to hang out hoping to find him. She felt like she had just been handed a death sentence that would take her away from her family. She had nothing to lose if she would take him off this earth, and at least that would ensure Tracey wouldn't be able to harm another person with his deceitful ways.

The anger was just the first wave. Depression came next. Momma stopped coming out of her room for a while. She wallowed in the belief that she would not be around to watch the rest of her children grow up, meet the rest of her grand-children. She sat and cried with me, telling me about all of the things that she had prayed she would be able to do with her children. She wanted to sew my prom dress for me, to make all of her girls' wedding dresses, to see all of our graduations, and be there for our wedding days. It took her a long time to come out of that fog. You couldn't have told her at the time, but she needn't have worried. Momma was going to hit every one of the goals on her list. She would live with that issue of blood for more than twenty years, and ultimately it would not even be the thing that took her from us.

All told, Momma spent an entire year not leaving her house. She moped, yes. But she also prayed and worked to get her strength back. Finally, around Thanksgiving, she called her whole family together to let us in on what she had been dealing with. Sharing her diagnosis helped, too. Now that all of her children understood what she was up against, Momma could lean on them and accept their support. This was also a time in her life when she repented for so many mistakes, asking God for forgiveness and to cover her. She started to walk with God in a whole different way and held herself like a woman saved. Her transition might not have been as obvious to others, after all Momma never really swore or drank around the house in front of any of us. But it was clear to her children.

As a woman now, when I hear pastors talk about "the woman with the issue of blood," in Luke 8:43 who had no name, I immediately compare her to my mom. The woman in the Bible heard about how Jesus was healing and performing miracles. She thought if she could just get to Him and touch the tassel or the hem of his garment, she would be healed from this bleeding she had suffered with for over a decade. But when she goes to meet Jesus, the woman falls through a crowd of people who judge her and do not want to have her company at all because of her issue. Still, she is able to touch Jesus's garment, and she is indeed healed.

My mom was counting on divine healing, too. For the first twelve years after her diagnosis, she refused medication because she believed in her heart that God would heal her and wouldn't let her die from this issue. I'm here to witness that God didn't let her die from it. For almost twenty years she was able to thrive, to watch us all grow up. She ran through the crowd being judged and she reached for God, by showing up and sharing His word to the people in her community and as she did *His* work, *He* gave her healing. That's how she started coming back to life, through her faith in God.

CHAPTER 6

Telling My Truth

*"The thing you fear most has no power. Your fear of it is what
has the power. Facing the truth really will set you free."*

—OPRAH WINFREY

Summers in Chicago were good for so many reasons. But as
I got a little older there was a big new one: money. I'm not a
materialistic person. But from the time I was able to do odd
jobs for family members I have felt called to make money.
It's a symbol of freedom, security, and independence, and
all three of those sound pretty good to me. So, I appreciated
when those trips started to come with the opportunity to
make money. I would help out whomever, however I could.
I would save some of my money, but much of it I would
spend getting ready for the school year. No longer did I
start each September in hand-me-downs and out-of-style
pieces. I wasn't able to afford every piece that I wanted. But

I could certainly get my hair and nails done, and have shoes, and clothes that marked me as someone who cared about her appearance and knew how to take care of herself. I had started to feel like someone you would never believe had to shake roaches out of her jackets every morning.

The summer I was twelve, I had never been more ready to make some cash so that I could head back in the fall in style. The girls in my neighborhood had started to feel like they were grown, and while I didn't want to keep up with them on the letting-boys-take-liberties front, I was very motivated to keep up with them on the fashion front. So, when I packed up and kissed Momma goodbye that June, I didn't expect to come back a changed person, only a better dressed one.

My visit unfolded as it normally did, with so many wonderful memories made with my sisters and brothers. I was grateful to help my extended family as well, catching up with and caring for my godmother, my grandmother's sister, and all the other ladies I waited all year to spend time with. The days passed quickly, and soon we had made it to a Sunday in the middle of the summer. Elder Charles was planning to attend a church convention, which in our faith in Chicago really just meant a gathering of congregants heading out to a church that they don't normally attend. He asked me if I would like to go with him. I was always up for exploring a new church, but I was especially excited at the prospect of a whole day out alone with Elder Charles. It wasn't often that

I got one of my older siblings all to myself for hours on end. That went double this particular summer for Elder Charles, because he had found himself a serious girlfriend. So, while he still certainly had time for me during my visit, he wasn't doling out day trips for just the two of us too regularly. My brother had also just signed up to enlist in the navy, so I was preparing for that new phase in our relationship. All of this made me eager to accept his invitation and hit the road.

We spent a half hour or forty-five minutes on the road since everywhere you go in Chicago takes at least that long. As we got closer to the church, we were visiting it was clear we were going to have some time to kill before we needed to arrive. Elder Charles pulled into the parking lot of a Dunkin' Donuts near our destination and told me he wanted to have a talk. He said to me, "I want you to know that you can trust me. And you know that I love you."

I said that, of course, I knew that, because, duh, and asked him what it was he wanted to talk about.

"I have a question I want to ask you," he went on, "but first I want to tell you a story."

"Ah, okay."

"You know I made some new friends over the past year. You've gotten to spend some time with some of them. Well,

I asked one of those friends if I can share something with you that's really personal but which I think it would be good for you to hear. When I first started hanging out with this friend, they trusted me with a story from their childhood that has impacted the person they are today. They told me about a situation when she was little where she was molested by someone in her life. And it hurt my feelings, you know, just to hear about it. But she trusted me and told me that, and that also made me feel proud. I was really glad that she felt that I could be part of her healing."

He looked at me then, seeming to judge whether I was about to freak out and bolt from the car into the empty parking lot. Then he kept going.

"And I'm sharing it with you because I want you to know at this age you are growing, your body's changing, and people will try to come on to you and do things to you. But I want you to know that your body is sacred. Don't let anyone do anything to you that they shouldn't be doing. I want you to protect yourself at all times. And don't hesitate to let someone know if someone's doing something to you that they shouldn't be doing."

Elder Charles stopped again, and this time he swallowed hard.

"Okay, that leads me to this question. And I want you to be honest with me."

I said, "Okay," but before he could even get the question out, I burst into tears. As I sobbed, he told me that he could tell that there was something that I needed to talk about and asked me if someone had put their hands on me.

Then he surprised me. He said, "Wipe your face. Wipe your face. Don't you dare cry. Tell me what's going on so I can help you fix it. Do you want me to name people? Or do you want me to ask about categories of people?"

I nodded to the latter, and he started with, "Was it anybody who lives in the household with you?" I shook my head.

"Was it any of the boyfriends or something like that?" I nodded.

"Tracey," he said. I looked up and closed my eyes and looked out the window. And he closed his eyes, too.

"I want to ask you because it's very important: What has he done to you? Did he touch you inappropriately? Kissed you?"

As innocent as I was, I didn't know any way to describe what he had done to me without walking through both of the assaults in full detail. So that's what I did. He promised me that I could trust him with this information, and that he would help me to deal with it. Then we dried our eyes and headed to church. The rest of the visit passed pleasantly, and

I had such a lightness about me having finally set this burden down in front of my brother. It's hard to believe, but I felt so completely wiped clean by the way Elder Charles had talked me through my pain that I actually forgot about our conversation. I let it go and focused on all the things that I loved about my summers away.

HOME AGAIN

The summer drew to a close and it was as hard as ever to say goodbye to my Chicago crew. Leaving Elder Charles was that much harder because of his enlistment. But I was also thrilled to be going home. I missed Momma, our house, our block, my friends, and my brothers. At home things seemed normal, and everyone was happy to have me back.

My friends had been coming by our house looking for me while I was gone. They told me Bronson would answer the door and report that I had moved out of town and wasn't coming back. That didn't stop them from still ringing the doorbell to see if I would answer. Bronson thought he was pretty funny as he laughed about this while I yelled at him.

After I had been home about a week or so, Momma told me one morning, "We've got an appointment today. I want you to go with me."

I wasn't thrilled. I had planned to spend the day catching

up with friends. But I also wasn't worried. I had started my period that summer, so I figured it was probably something to do with menstruation. When we pulled into the lot for the medical complex, though, Momma turned to me in her seat, and I started to feel anxious.

"Tiyah, I want to ask you something," she said and, at this point, I could feel the shivers coming down my shoulders because I knew what she was about to ask me. I was not lying anymore, though. I was finished covering up for him. So, I just blurted out my truth.

And I'll tell you, my mom knocked it out of the park. Once she knew, she did everything right, at least for what I needed. She cured me as a woman, and I thank her for that. She apologized to me for not preventing it, for bringing that man into our lives, and for not seeing who he was and how he had changed me. She asked questions, she told me it was not my fault, and she told me that it changed nothing about who I was as a girl, nor would it change who I became as a woman. She put me back together the moment she knew.

She kept looking at me in that car, saying, "I'm sorry. I'm so sorry." Then, she told me that she promised she was not going to go look for Tracey. At the time, I wondered why she said that. Later, my brother explained that back when Momma received her diagnosis, she had rolled around for days searching for Tracey. She hit all of his regular haunts, ready to take him out, to give her life to get back at him. This time, she was telling me that she was not going to let herself go to that place.

"I'm going to let God bring him to me." She knew that the things that were done in the dark would eventually come to light. We talked about going to the police, but I didn't want to be in court and on the news, and she respected that.

"It's about how you feel," Momma assured me. And I knew deep down that I could trust that. I started crying, she started crying, and then she told me why we were really here for this appointment.

"Tiyah, the blood problem I have, it came from Tracey. Because of what he did to you, I'm worried that you could have this, too. And so, it's crucial that we go and talk to the doctor, go through some tests, and find out what we're dealing with."

I still had no idea what this really meant. I didn't understand that we hadn't had intercourse, and that the chances of my having contracted something were incredibly low. I knew he had touched me. I knew some sort of liquid had been in my underwear. And I knew I was scared and relieved all at once. Momma hugged me and was kissing me on my forehead and told me she had been praying all week long. Before we got out of the car, we prayed together for a good result from the tests.

Inside, the nurse talked to me briefly about blood draws and how long it would take to hear back about my results. After the appointment, Momma drove me to my friend's house and told me she didn't want me to think about this anymore today. She told me to be a kid for the rest of the day. She didn't want this to mess up my childhood any more than it already had.

Then, Momma looked me in the eye and said, "Nobody will ever hurt you again. I just could kill Tracey if I saw him right now, but I'm not going to go look for him this time. I'm asking God to bring him to me."

God doesn't love drama, so it was ironic that, a year later, he chose Mother's Day as the day to answer Momma's prayer. Tracey showed up on her doorstep with flowers while two of my brothers were visiting from Chicago, and Bronson and Daniel were home. I was at my friend Shana's house, who lived behind us, and my brother Bronson was sent over to bring me back.

"Momma wants you right now," he told me, without explaining why. As I started to protest, he told me it was serious, and I needed to come immediately.

Doeboy was staying with us while recovering from being shot; he was in a wheelchair and was the first one I saw as I walked into the house. He looked at me strangely. I passed Elder Charles in the dining area, wearing the same look on his face that he had when I told him that I had been abused.

As soon as I made it far enough into the house to see the kitchen, I saw Precious looking right at me. I turned the corner and there was Momma by the stove. Daniel and a friend were by the back door, posted up like guards, but avoiding looking at me.

And then I saw him: perched by our kitchen table was Tracey.

Immediately, I felt like that little girl again. I started shaking and my whole body went cold. Precious saw it, and she said, "Oh, no. Oh, no. You don't have to be ashamed today. You are going to stand here, flat-footed, and tell him what you told us."

Momma agreed. "You don't have to be afraid today. Just tell him what you told us."

I turned to Tracey and did as I was told. "You used to touch me," I forced out.

He was a big liar. So, of course, he turned to my mom and said, "Hattie, she's lying."

Momma shut him right down. "This isn't your time to talk. You're done talking." Then she turned to me and said, "You tell him everything that you told us."

This time, it all just flowed out of me like water. I said, "You used to touch me; you did it since we've lived here, you did

it back in Chicago. You left something behind in my panties."
I went through everything that had happened. And Tracey
didn't call me a liar again after that.

He turned to Momma and said, "I'm sorry, Hattie. I'm so
sorry."

Momma ignored him and told me, "Okay, you can go back
outside now."

As I turned to walk out, Momma slid a pan off the stove,
holding it like she couldn't wait to swing it. The moment I
made it to the dining room, I heard that pan slam right into
the back of Tracey's head, and he started screaming. That
initial pan hit was critical for me because now I felt sorry
for him. I thought, "Oh, they're about to tear you up in here."

I was right. As I continued toward the front of the house, I
heard Momma say to Daniel and his friend, "Do whatever
you want to him, but try not to get blood on yourselves."

Out on the front porch, I sat myself down next to Bronson
and started crying.

"Don't feel sorry for the dude," he told me.

A minute later, Jackson's car swung onto our block. He
jumped out while it was practically still moving.

"You know, you could have told me," he said to me as he flew up the stairs, grabbing the two-by-four we kept by the door for security on the way. I heard Jackson and the other boys move Tracey to the basement, and five long minutes of screaming followed. Then Tracey appeared at the door, looking like the meat was hanging out of his head, practically walking into the wall. Momma followed close behind and clearly didn't care that he was hurting.

"You don't know how to get out? You need some more help?" she asked.

Tracey promptly hurled himself off the porch, flipped over the banister, and just kept moving. He wanted to get away from that lady and her house as fast as he could. As soon as Tracey was out of sight, Bronson turned to me and said, "Okay, go back and play. You don't need to stay at the house now."

Just like that, it was all over for him. It took me a little longer to recover from Tracey's visit. I worried for a while that I would come home and find him in the kitchen again, or that he would show up at my bus stop. Until, one day, I mentioned my concerns to Momma.

"Don't worry about that," she said, without a trace of doubt. "Believe me, he's not that stupid." And I *did* believe her. I let the worry that I would ever have to see Tracey again go, for good.

A NEGATIVE TEST

Several days after I had my blood drawn, we finally got word about my test.

I was down the street, at the corner of 26th, getting ready to walk somewhere with my friends. My sister ran down to stop me and deliver the news. Precious held an envelope in her hand and said, "Tiyah, the test was negative!" I started crying and she held me. This was such a relief for an eleven-year-old child.

When Momma was first diagnosed, she had told us that she had a death sentence. I had thought about that each day that I waited for my results, feeling like maybe I had that same death sentence hanging over my head.

Now, I wanted to fall to the ground at the corner of this busy street because of the physical relief that I felt. I had tested negative! We both cried while we hugged and thanked God. Then, Precious told me to wipe my eyes, and get on going to wherever it was I had been headed.

"I just wanted to tell you right away once I saw that envelope. I wanted to remind you that God is good. God came through for you, Sis."

Precious had pulled me aside from my friends, and when I rejoined them, they all wanted to know, "What happened? What's wrong?"

I wasn't sharing my news. I just told them that we had gotten some happy information and everything was fine. They let it drop, and we were back on our way.

CHAPTER 7

Knowing My Worth

"Everything that happens to you is a reflection of what you believe about yourself. We cannot outperform our level of self-esteem. We cannot draw to ourselves more than we think we are worth."

—IYANLA VANZANT

From the day I told Momma about the Monster, I walked differently. My shame was gone, and so was my fear. I had a new sense of myself and my worth, and it came just in time to carry me into puberty armed with the ability to say, "No," until the exact moment that I was ready to say, "Yes."

I also had something from the before times start to come back to me. It didn't happen overnight, but I started to reclaim some of the physical ease that I'd had with my brothers. As long as I can remember, I've known that the way my siblings and I are together is something special.

It's pretty unusual to have so many grown siblings wanting to dote on you. In some families that I know, the littlest kid feels left out, or like they're always trying to keep up. I never felt that way. I was never made to feel like a fifth wheel with the bigger children just because they're so much older than me. Instead, I was the baby who everyone wanted to hold, pick up, walk to the store, play mama to. I know they found happiness when they saw me, and I carried that with me. It's easy to see where I'm lucky there.

The way my younger brothers were with me was different since we're so close in age. But it was always just as close, easy, and fun.

Before the Monster, my youngest brother and I were the most physical together. We were each other's favorite playmates; whether outside racing, or inside play fighting, we were always up to something together. If there weren't enough beds for everyone staying the night, we shared a bed or the sofa. And even on regular nights I ended up in his bed if I got scared.

With all of my brothers, I had enjoyed total physical and emotional comfort. I had no awareness of my body as a thing I needed to hide, or a thing I should be ashamed of. I felt completely worthy of their love; I wanted them to see me exactly as I am because that's the Tiyah they adore. Why on earth would I want to hide her from them?

SAYING GOODBYE TO BEING SEEN

After the assaults, nothing about how my brothers felt about me changed at all. It hasn't to this day. In the depth of my hardest moments, I didn't doubt that they loved me. But I did lose for a while how simple it all was for me.

I lost how unbothered I was by being completely seen by my brothers. Once everything changed, I felt that I needed to hide. So, I no longer wanted to be see-through in front of my brothers. Inside, I didn't think I was the Tiyah they thought I was anymore.

I lost the complete unawareness of my body as anything other than a beautiful vessel, arms to hug those I loved with. And I gained an understanding that not all physical touch was a good or safe thing.

My memories of those "before days" are of feeling secure, serene, and relaxed. I never felt wrong or bad. And I was as trusting as you could be. I knew that I could trust my brothers completely. I knew they would never do anything to hurt me, certainly not in the manner I was about to be injured. In fact, I didn't even know that possibility existed, to be honest. My young brain never could have conceived of any family member, or friend, or person who had been taken in by my mom's goodness, wanting anything from my body that was bad.

It hadn't occurred to my mom either, really. Back then, she

had told me not to let any boys mess with me, and to come tell her if they tried anything. But I don't think Momma could imagine that it was time to have a frank and pointed conversation with her seven-year-old daughter about how to protect her body from a predator. Or explain to her that a grown man she knew might try to turn her trusting nature against her.

Once I was unburdened, I wasn't magically healed, but God did start right away to set me on that path. And it was easiest with my brothers. Feeling their arms around me started to feel normal again, and I was more grateful for that change than I can describe.

ACTING GROWN

At this point, some of my friends were sexually active. They told me all about it, and I would listen without judgment. It just wasn't for me. I had a whole new level of respect for myself, with everything that I had come through, and how my mother and my brother had raised me up and valued me. And that's what made me hold onto my virginity until I was ready. I for sure wasn't ready at thirteen. That didn't make the boys in our group very happy, of course. I had a friend who would go visit a certain boy, and when they were ready to get down to business I would clear out and go wait in the alley beside his house while they were down in his basement. I spent a lot of time in alleys over the next few years. But it was fine. I didn't begrudge her the experiences she was having. But I also wasn't jealous, wishing it was me. God had sent me through a different set of circumstances, and I just wasn't carefree with my body or my soul in the way many my age were. I didn't think that it made me better than anyone. But I also wasn't interested in being talked out of what I was committed to. I would be waiting in the alley if anyone needed me.

I was so glad that Momma had made it clear to me that you don't have to do everything that your friends are doing at that moment. If a boy is not going to talk to you because you're not saying okay to what he wants, you don't need him. And if your friends are ready for things you're not, that's fine. Let them do their thing. You do yours. And just love each other through it. Momma made sure I understood.

And I tried to share that understanding when I saw that some of the girls I ran with wanted boys to like them so much that they were ready to do things they weren't into just to make that happen. I didn't care if my friends wanted to act on their own impulses. But I wasn't about to let them believe that any man could pressure them to give away something they didn't want to.

My renewed self-worth and iron-clad sense of self didn't make me perfect, to be clear. I still made plenty of mistakes as a teenager and made even more once I became an adult. I wish I could get away with not putting this particular example in the book, but every one of my siblings has made it clear they expect it be in here. It's a story my sister makes sure she tells at every gathering.

I failed when I tried to smoke pot for the first time. I had a friend whose mom smoked both cigarettes and drugs. So, they knew drug dealers and where we could purchase weed. Several of my friends liked to smoke from time to time, but I wasn't interested. They never pushed me, and that was that. Until one day I just felt like giving it a whirl. I told them, "Okay, let's see what you're so hung up on."

I smoked. Nothing happened. I felt nothing. It just somehow…didn't work. One more sign that weed wasn't for Atiyah, I guessed!

Then, two months later, we were down the street at my friend's house on another block. She and her grandma were getting ready to smoke. And I thought, "Heck, let me give it another try." I took a couple of puffs, expecting nothing, and I immediately felt a shift in my body. Okay. Well, that's weird. Within minutes I was acting so goofy. I was running around the house with my friend's younger sister acting childish and silly. Her mom was there, and this was a woman who did hard drugs, and was perpetually short on cash, so I was always handing her a little money. On this day, as I'm acting a fool with her younger daughter, she comes up and asks me,

"Atiyah, you have some money? Let me have a few dollars to go to the store and get some beer."

Now, on a normal day that would have been a slam-dunk for my friend's mom. I would have handed the money over without hesitation. But today, I was high for the first time in my life. And high Atiyah was also hungry for an ice cream sandwich! So, I said, "Well, no. I only have a dollar. And I'm going to get me an ice cream sandwich with that dollar because it's mine, and I have the munchies now."

That was the wrong answer because this woman was evil. And she had really wanted that beer. Within fifteen minutes the fallout of my refusal came home to roost. We all heard *boom, boom, boom, boom, boom, boom, boom, boom.*

My friend went to answer the door and came back ashen faced. She told me, "Atiyah, your mom is at the front door."

High Atiyah decided some water on my face would sober me right up, so I rushed to the bathroom and tossed water at myself, not realizing I was actually dousing my whole head. I took my wet head to the front of the house, where the front door was closed and presumably Momma was waiting outside. I flung that door open and walked straight out to start explaining to Momma that, despite what she may have heard from that turncoat, drug-hunting mom of my friend, I was presently sober as a judge and I…missed the first step entirely. I fell straight toward my Momma, my eyes wide and shocked, looking right into hers.

Two of my brothers were there, as was one of my sisters (who tells the story often…) standing behind Momma. All four of them were standing in alignment from the door to the sidewalk. I thought I was going to die right where I stood.

Momma held my gaze and said, "Atiyah, have you been smoking?"

"No," I answered quickly.

"I'm going to ask you one more time. Have you been smoking?"

And this time I said, "Yes." I think she was already on to me, though…

My friend's mother took the heat off me for a bit when she made the grand mistake of stepping up to Momma, saying, "You should have known; you have to look in her eyes more often."

Momma was insulted, and also couldn't believe the gall of that woman, since she was the one who had allowed this nonsense in the first place. Running her mouth like that earned my friend's mom a whooping from Momma. She ran off as soon as she could get free from Momma, calling her crazy as she retreated.

When we got home, I was put on restriction until the new millennium. My mom knew that a whooping wasn't going to work for me. She needed to take my freedom in order to truly punish me. So, I was allowed no friends, no phone calls, and no time outside. And then that cake got frosted with a bit of embarrassment, to really drive my punishment home.

I had a friend from school, Chanelle, who wasn't from the neighborhood, who only knew me from school. So Chanelle knew only the really good me; she didn't know the hood me at all. She still laughs today about the time she came looking for me during that period of punishment. She got to the door and was met by my sister who told her to go home.

"You won't see Tiyah for a long, long time."

I was staring at her from the top of the staircase like I was terrified. And Chanelle just waved sadly up to me, mouthing, *goodbye,* like she knew I was about to die.

CHAPTER 8

Teen Mom on Welfare

"Shame cannot survive being spoken," Brown says. "It cannot survive empathy."

—DR. BRENÉ BROWN

The first time I pushed a baby carriage for one of my classmates I was fourteen. That's when my friends started having babies. The closest was my girlfriend whom I had met in sixth grade. She lived around the corner from me, and from the time we met we were by each other's houses every day, walking back and forth, singing and dancing, and just having fun together. At fourteen, I watched her grow into an amazing mother.

She was hardly the only one. As friend after friend came

by my house with their little babies as teenagers, Momma would just say, "Oh, you're a mother now, huh? Well, you better be. You better be a mother now, now that you have this precious little one."

Momma had her first baby at fifteen, too, so while other parents might have looked down on them, she was nothing but supportive, never speaking a negative word.

In our neighborhood, making it to adulthood without having had a baby was a real accomplishment. As I approached eighteen having never been pregnant, I felt pretty much like citizen of the year.

I had been dating the same boy since I was fifteen, and we had only recently started sleeping together. He was my first and only, and we were madly in love. Not everyone thought it was a fine romance, however. This relationship, in fact, had broken my brother Bronson's heart. Kevin was his friend from the time they were both ten years old. And over time Kevin morphed into being a friend of mine, too. We walked to the store together; we talked a lot about what was going on at school. And around the time I was fourteen, I realized friendship had turned into a huge crush.

My brother was so mad that I dated him. I should have respected that boundary. My brother wasn't in charge of whom I dated, but he had my best interests fully in mind and he knew things about his friend that I didn't. At the end of the day, I should have listened.

I didn't listen, though, because I was sixteen and hopped-up on first love and hormones. Those are the same factors I blamed, coincidentally, when Kevin and I learned just shy of me turning eighteen that we were expecting a baby.

I was scared to tell Momma that I was pregnant. Of course, I knew that she was going to be supportive. I had seen the way that she was with my friends. I just didn't want her to be disappointed in me. But she was also the person I knew would be able to help me the most, so I needed to fill her in. First, I told my sister Peaches.

At this point, Peaches was married and had moved out... sort of! She lived with her husband and two children on the top level of our duplex. The back door to their unit and the back door to our unit were both always left open. That meant that both families could come and go as they pleased from the two homes. As soon as I found out I was going to have a baby, I popped upstairs to Peaches for advice. She coached me to tell Momma right away, so that I could get the proper help as needed.

When I told Momma, she said. "You being pregnant is okay. You didn't have to be scared to tell me because you know I had my first child young, too. The thing I want to make sure that you understand from the start, Atiyah, is that a baby doesn't mess up your life. It's not something to regret. But you certainly can mess up a child's life. So, you need to prepare yourself to do right by them. The baby's gonna be fine. The baby is easy. You need to prepare yourself not to mess up that *child's* life."

That advice stuck with me, and it motivated me to be ready not just for the baby's arrival, but for actual parenting. Kevin and I started getting excited about the pregnancy once my mom knew and had calmed me down. I was so grateful to Momma for getting my head right about not seeing this baby with any regret. Thanks to her, when I pushed that baby out at eighteen, I was crying happy tears, praising God, and thanking Jesus. I didn't know I could pray so hard.

My friend Cara was a great support as I got ready for parenthood, too. She was a year ahead of me in high school, and we hung out almost every day during school. When she was nineteen, she and a friend of my brother's had a baby, and I was so impressed with how she handled it. When I got pregnant, Cara had me come to her same doctor, and walked me through so many of the girl-to-girl things you need to talk about during pregnancy. She stayed with us from time to time, and we were like sisters. I know that Cara, along with the rest of my close good friends, were sent by God to help me through this lifetime.

It dampened that happy period when my brother and I stopped

talking for five months. I had delayed telling him about my pregnancy for as long as I could, hoping to at least get through my high school graduation before I dropped that bomb on him. As it happened, a friend's mom would ruin that one for me. She let it slip as we were taking graduation photos at the ceremony. It was a terrible way for him to find out, and the fact that he wasn't hearing it from me in private made everything that much worse. Bronson was just so angry at me that I wouldn't listen and felt like I wasn't allowing him to protect me. Instead, I had taken his objections all along as a sign that he didn't understand how much Kevin loved me. Bronson had seen Kevin with other girls, and it wasn't the treatment he wanted for me. Instead of hearing that my brother knew something about this man that I didn't and wanted a certain level of treatment for me when I became someone's wife, I just wanted to prove Kevin loved me more than the others that had come before.

I made him wait a whole year before we were intimate. I made him jump through all these stupid hoops. I would tell Kevin he had to catch a cab over on his side of town and walk me to the other side of town. I would call and say I was hungry and ask if he could take the bus over and bring me something to eat. I just made him do all kinds of weird stuff to see what all I could get him to do for me. I was trying to prove to my brother, "Look at all this stuff he's trying to do for me. He never did that for the other girls."

After we found out I was pregnant, I was still living with Momma, but I didn't want to bring the baby home to that house. I was just obsessed with getting out of that back room with my baby. I started investigating my options and found a low-income apartment where they set the rent based on what you made. I was able to get approved for the apartment and had a move-in date that was well before my due date. I was so happy!

Years earlier, I had talked my way into a job at Walgreens, which meant I had some money saved up to help pay for the apartment. When I was a high school junior, I had called up the store and said, "Hi, I have an interview scheduled for tomorrow and I just wanted to verify the time."

And a manager got on the line and was like, "You have an interview, do you? What's your name?" I told him my name, and he let me know that he was well aware that I did not, in fact, have an interview tomorrow. He knew this for a fact because he had set all of the appointments himself, and he had most certainly not called anyone by my name. He told me that he was impressed with how scrappy and determined I was and agreed to interview me just the same.

I had been working as a shampoo girl for my sister all through high school, making $5 a head, but now I was ready for steady employment. My interview went well, and I ended up working at Walgreens for two full years. I kept working at Walgreens for as long as I could during my pregnancy until I couldn't stand on my feet long enough to work a full shift.

When moving day arrived, I felt so proud of myself. Kevin was happy about the apartment, too, but his name wasn't on the lease, and he hadn't been the one working for it. That first night, I didn't have any furniture loaded in, so I slept on the floor of my new apartment. I had asked Kevin to stay over with me, but he wasn't impressed by the lack of creature comforts. "I'll come over in the morning." I didn't like that answer. He left me there, pregnant, sleeping on the floor by myself, because just being with me wasn't enough to warrant sleeping somewhere less than comfortable.

The moment my furniture came, though, he was happy to kick back and stay the night. But I could not let his behavior the night before go that easily. We didn't break up over the incident, but I count it as the first time I glimpsed the real kind of partner he was going to be for me. And it wasn't pretty.

Soon after my son arrived, I started a medical assistant program. It was a lot to do with a newborn, but I was committed to making a better life for our family. I had hoped I would be able to rely on Kevin to help financially and with childcare, but he always seemed to be unavailable when I needed coverage for my night classes. And he seemed to always be coming up short when I needed him to pitch in on essentials for our baby. I started to really see that Kevin didn't want to help with the bills. He wasn't concerned about getting an education so that he could put more money toward his child's life. That was what I was worried about. But Kevin was showing me he just wasn't.

Then the cheating started. Kevin got stuck in an obvious lie more than one time. But there was one incident where I really caught him red-handed. It happened when we were living in the last home we shared together, and my son had just turned three. Kevin had just quit a good-paying job after only a few weeks, which had me upset with him. I had helped him get this job, filling out his application, and coaching him through his interview so that he could land this role that could have been so good for us. Thanks to me, at twenty he had been hired by Harley-Davidson, making $16 an hour without a high school diploma.

As intelligent as he was, Kevin just didn't have the drive to complete his education and think about the future for his son at that time. I was thinking about the future for both of us, and that was draining. Thank God I had my mom; Momma never said no to her grandson being dropped off, whether it was Kevin or me doing the asking. She said she didn't want me to ask anyone else, or ever have him in danger. She would rather keep him because she knew he was safe.

That meant that I was able to go out there and work on my education and make money for our little family. But I was in it on my own. Kevin would make some money moves to buy my son shoes and nice clothes here and there, but that wasn't enough for me. At his core, he didn't want to work; he wanted to do street things and risk me having to tie my life down for six or seven years when he went away. As much as it can sometimes be flattering to have a man be able to buy you things because he's out there making money in a way that he shouldn't, it wasn't worth the risk to me, certainly not now that I was a mother. I wanted Kevin to want something different in the same way that I did. And I should have seen sooner that he just didn't. It took catching him cheating to finally break us up.

On that day that I caught Kevin cheating, I was headed off to work and my son was supposed to be with his father after his half day of preschool. I ended up coming back home early and I took a strange way home. I can't tell you why, but I took a road I never took; it's a road Kevin would never expect me to be on, at a time he would never expect me to be around. And as I was going down that street, I saw our car coming toward me, with some strange woman in the passenger's seat. I whipped around and headed back in the direction they were going and saw Kevin had pulled into a gas station. The woman had jumped out of the car and started walking down an alley across the street. I flew out of my car and went after her.

"Excuse me? Hello? Yes, excuse me!" I yelled toward her unabashedly as I gained on her. "Hi! Miss! Yes, you! Hello? Why were you riding in my car?"

That got her and she turned and said, "I was in Kevin's car."

Oh, were you now? At least we've confirmed it was you in there with my boyfriend.

"No, you were in my car," I told her. "You were in my car with my son's father, and I would like to know why."

She told me that she was his cousin, that she lived on the other side of town, and they were just catching up because they hadn't seen each other in a while. Yeah, it must have been *quite* a while. I've been knowing this boy since I was eight years old, and I've never seen this woman before, but she's supposed to be a local cousin? She picked the wrong person for her story that day.

But I didn't get feisty with her or try to chase her lies. I turned on my heel and walked back across to Kevin to see if they had coordinated their stories. Sure enough, Kevin hit me with the same nonsense.

"If that's your cousin, take me to her mama's house right now and introduce me," I countered.

He didn't know what to do with that, so we just got in the car and Kevin started driving. He looked like a deer caught in the headlights, just driving on autopilot. He took me to this other area of town and he pulled up and got out He called this woman out onto the porch of her house. I sat there in the car, watching them talk animatedly. Honestly, he was probably begging her to tell me she was his auntie. But the two of them were standing out there way too long for this to be a family member you're about to introduce me to.

I started to break. You want me to be stupid? Play dumb and listen to your story? I can't be stupid. I'm not even going to try to figure out how long you guys have been creeping and sneaking. And I'm not going to listen to this woman, who looks like a crackhead, whom you're trying to pass off as some unknown auntie. I pulled off on her when she started coming down to the car. I just didn't have it in me to play this game anymore, to even listen to the lie she had just been convinced to come down and tell me.

Later, he came clean. Kevin finally admitted she wasn't his cousin, something I knew as soon as I had pulled up on her. Looking back, this was the type of stuff my brother knew. He was afraid of his sister being treated this way. I stayed longer than I should have because I knew Kevin loved his son. He would take him everywhere he went. On that day, though, I was finally ready to see the whole picture. I told Kevin that he was taking my kindness for weakness, and that if we can't get along anymore, we have to get apart. His grandmother had said that quote to me before, and now I understood it. Finally, I snapped. I told him, "You're just not a man. You don't know how to be a man yet. And I'm not going to stay here any longer to try to teach you."

I told him to get out, but he wouldn't, so I moved back with my mom for a few months, and then he moved out, too. Now that he would have to pay the rent on his own, he didn't last long in the apartment. After six years, at twenty-one years old, we finally went our separate ways for good.

Kevin stayed involved with his son, but from then on, my son and I were on our own. It was an overwhelming lesson at the time: some people are in your life for only a season. They're not there forever, but they are there to teach you something.

Now that I was single, though, it didn't feel all that different. I realized I had been carrying the full burden of parenthood on my own already and that helped me believe I could continue to provide for us on my own. And it helped lift my spirits that my mom loved having me back home for that time. She was so happy to have my friends back in the mix, catching up with them, these five whom I had been friends with forever. There we were, back at Momma's house again, getting dressed to go out, or just hanging out. She would enjoy spending time with us and laugh at us, "being grown." My older brother Hardy had bought my mom a new home located off the street we grew up on and missed so much. I stayed with her there for a month and my son was so happy. He would go get in the bed with her at night and leave me; I didn't realize the bond they had until I sat still long enough to see just how crazy about his grandmother he truly was.

I did feel sadness during that time that my first born would grow up in a household without his father. But I was learning that sometimes it takes more than one try to break a generational curse.

My second chance at doing just that came along a whole lot faster than anyone thought it would, including me. Soon after Kevin and I broke up, I met Lukas. We started dating fast and got married a mere year and a half after the breakup.

We rushed and had a wedding less than two years after we'd met, inviting family and friends to celebrate with us in Las Vegas. It all felt so right, but it also felt wrong. After the ceremony, getting on a roller coaster, I threw up. Soon we realized why: there was already a third party in this new marriage of ours.

That marriage brought me a beautiful daughter, but anyone paying attention could tell that it wasn't built to last. I had rushed into it too quickly without healing from the breakup with Kevin or even giving myself time to adjust to new motherhood. Still, I can't blame the failure of that marriage on timing, really. It wasn't love. And I fooled myself into thinking it was. Speaking for both women and men, we all know when we are being loved right and we definitely know when something isn't right. It's in that moment that we have to make the right decision. I believe in second chances. But does real love actually take eight or nine chances to prove itself, when it's hurting you mentally and physically? I think it does not.

Lukas had never been physical with me, during most of our relationship, but I had heard he had been before. One of his exes was persistent in letting me know he hit her before, and I would listen, but never took action. Until one day when Lukas questioned me about my son's father and we got into a big physical altercation. I knew then by the way he handled me he couldn't love me; it had to be lust. But in that same moment, after he came from the hospital where he needed stitches, he realized I wasn't the one to play with either. There was nothing left to salvage, and to be honest, neither one of us really knew the other all that well as our marriage ended.

While my personal life was in constant flux and I seemed uniquely qualified to choose highly unsuitable partners, my work life was taking off. I had left Walgreens and taken a job in a nursing home while I worked on my medical assistant degree. With that degree, I moved into a position at a hospital.

I saw a pattern starting to develop that concerned me. I had moved through my teens and early twenties, two relationships, and two pregnancies keeping my work goals and my marriage goals separate. I hadn't required either of the men in my life to be partners in the life I hoped to build for our children. Neither of them had stepped up to provide for me, or my kids, and that was on them. But was I partially responsible for the fact that neither man saw me as interested in building a solid financial house together. I was proud that I was independent, but did I come off as if I didn't want help from my partner, or was I too much of a caretaker in my relationships?

As I took steps to move out of my current marriage, it turned out I had already met the man who would help me answer those questions and learn to combine my family and professional goals.

CHAPTER 9

Entrepreneurship

"A woman's heart must be so hidden in God that a man must seek Him to find her."

—MAYA ANGELOU

You've gotten a front-row seat to some spectacularly bad relationship decisions. And you got to ride-along as I embarrassed myself the first time I got baked. But I promise you those aren't the only times I've been reckless and childish. When I was fifteen, for instance, I started driving without a license. I had places that I wanted to go, and access to a car, so I just got in and went.

My son got his license this year, and it was so emotional for me. I didn't realize why at first, until I thought about what it meant not just for him, but the whole family line. It felt to me like my son had broken a generational curse of mine: of doing things the wrong way because you're ready now and want to get what you think is next in your life as quickly as possible. I've done that with relationships both on the way in and the way out, and I'm working hard to learn not to do either. But I had forgotten how that decision to come at driving a car the wrong way almost limited my family's future.

When I was my son's age, I was driving illegally all the time.

The story of how I even had a car at the age of fifteen is actually a nice one. It was the beginning of so many things starting to change for my family and me. My mom had bought me a car for about $300; it was a small, red, two-door Dodge Shadow. I saw it sitting outside in front of the house and she said, "You like that car?" I told her I sure did, and she told me, "It's yours!"

I was so happy! I hugged Momma and she couldn't believe how appreciative I was for a Dodge Shadow. Are you kidding me? I didn't care! This was a car! Not to mention that this car had no scrapes or dents, and that made it perfect to me.

It didn't occur to me in that moment how God had started turning things around for me. I went from being the under-dog with nothing but a loving family and a great sense of humor, to so many new blessings. I now had a car. I had a sister now working as a cosmetologist who did my hair for me in a new style every two weeks. Plus, I had a job with her as her shampoo girl and a job for her boss cleaning the shop. She paid me well every week and gifted me real Coach bags and belts. Things had started to change. I was a high school student who could buy herself new shoes every week; I had new clothes to share with my friends. God started blessing this underdog in ways I couldn't even imagine. I would draw what I wanted to wear for my birthday and how my hair would lay, and just like that at sixteen I had nailed it! I was starting to write down my dreams and visions, manifesting them without even realizing it!

It also didn't occur to me that despite all of those blessings, one blessing I hadn't yet received was my actual license. So, when Momma gave me that car I started driving illegally. But I wasn't getting away with it. This wasn't something I was actually good at, driving illegally! No, at fifteen I began to amass an almost inconceivable stockpile of tickets for driving without a license. And I paid not a one of them. When, at the age of twenty, I wanted to buy a car to help me get to my job, I found that my mountains of unpaid tickets had not been kind to my credit rating and that I would have to place on pause any hope of being given a loan.

My son didn't try something like that. He's not the same person as his mom, so, of course, we can expect him to make different decisions and his own unique set of mistakes. But it's also not something that would occur to him because he has watched his mother make smart decisions financially during his childhood. And so, there's not a generational curse that he's inheriting on that front. In the same year that my son got a license to drive, in fact, my husband and I finished up the annual taxes for our business only to see that what was so recently a fledgling endeavor was worth $1.2 million in 2020. Making that happen just wasn't that hard to achieve once we were chasing the correct goals. And it makes me that much happier to know that, with my husband and me as role models, it will be all that much easier for our children to identify and chase their dreams.

Does it sound like I'm bragging when I tell you how well our business has been able to perform in such a short amount of time? Because claiming credit for that success rocket is the opposite of what I mean to do. I'll take credit all day for setting a great example for my son. And when he does great things, I'll happily take some credit for those as well. But strange as it may sound, I don't feel fully responsible for what's happened with our business. God chose to bless my husband and me with abundant professional growth just as soon as we stopped chasing a dream meant for someone else. Doing that's a great way to feel like a failure, though I certainly had to learn that lesson the hard way. That success isn't yours, so it won't come to you no matter how hard you toil. When you align your passion with what God has clearly called you to do, however, it falls into place easily.

It took me a lot of stops and starts to connect the dots

between my lifelong passion for caring for and learning from the elders in my community with my interest in healthcare. After high school, I looked at what my best friend had planned. She was ready to attend nursing school. That sounded reasonable, and I wanted the financial stability that she told me it might bring. So, I enrolled, too. But it was never the right path for me. I was chasing my friend's dream, even though it wasn't meant for me. Lucky for me, though, I still ended up in hospitals and nursing homes, spending time with elderly people who needed care and compassion. Through those moments, God was able to work in my heart and show me the exact role that truly called to me.

SHOW ME THE WAY

I was on break one afternoon at the nursing home and I just started doodling a business plan. I thought to myself, I want to open up my own group home. I love the work that I get to do with my patients here, and I know that there is such a need for spaces in group homes where patients can be as happy as they are here. But that requires the homes to be well run, by someone with a background in the medical caring profession, but also a genuine interest in making the elderly feel comfortable, engaged, and valued.

Something came over me that just told me this was what my community needed, and that I could do this myself.

One of the nurses asked, "What are you working on? You're always writing." So, I told her, and she told me that was going to be a hard sell. "The state isn't going to okay a site until you get approval from everyone in the neighborhood. Do you know how hard that is to do?"

I started to feel discouragement creep in, and I thought, you know, maybe I don't need to be working on this. I was making good money. I had good job security and a path to more money eventually. I should be grateful for what I had, even if it wasn't the perfect role for me. And just in the moment when I was about to let that wave of self-doubt pull me under, this respiratory therapist named Bill walked over to me.

He was about sixty-nine years old at the time. And, because God works in mysterious ways, he chose that day to sit down at my table after my friend the killjoy had gotten up to go.

"Tiyah," he asked, "What are you writing?" I sighed internally, because I wasn't ready to get my dream beaten up again for the second time in five minutes. I really just wanted to go in a corner and lick my wounds. But Bill was kind and earnest and I knew he was asking out of genuine interest, so I explained my idea another time.

Bill listened, nodding as I talked, then asked excitedly, "Great! I have something for you. I'm going to give you a book because I've been watching you. I bet you're ready to do something special."

The next day, not only did Bill bring the book for me, but he brought pictures of a dome house. He had built it with his own hands, a dream house for him, his wife, and their children. The book he wanted me to read was called *Dreaming with God*. He said, "You see this, you see this dome? I built this dome house. It has a fireplace, beds, a second level. I dreamed this with God and in three years my family lived there. Anything is possible. So, start reading. And when you finish that book, I've got another book for you." The books he had me read kept me motivated and showed me how achievable dreams are when you and God are pulling in the same direction. In the moment, I knew Bill was wonderful, but I'm not sure I realized what he truly was. Now I know that God will send you earthly angels when someone is trying to kill your dreams. Amen to that, and thank you, Bill.

TRUE PARTNERS

My next hurdle was that I couldn't open a group home until I could first buy a house. I had to bite the bullet and get my credit together because no one was going to give me a loan just yet. And I'm not sure I wouldn't still be struggling with that if I hadn't found my right partner in life. There's a reason my Momma called my husband a knight in shining armor. He came to help me become the woman I was meant to be and he put the time in long before we were anything more than friends.

I met Knight when I was still with my son's father. It would be a long time before we were romantic, but I certainly thought he was smooth from the start. He was living a fast life and I was not sure if I was going to go back and try to make it work with my son's dad. Still, Knight and I started talking. He was charming and so interesting to talk to, and even though we both still had so much personal growth to go through, I sensed he really was concerned about my well-being.

Case in point, when I told him that I was going to give it another shot with my son's father. He seemed disappointed, yet also worried. He wondered how I was going to do that after the nasty things I had told him were said. Would I be safe? Would my son and I be comfortable?

Knight was a ladies' man and I assumed he had a whole bunch of women stashed away somewhere, so I couldn't quite let myself take him seriously anyway. After I broke the news that I was going back to my relationship, Knight told me he would be out of town for a while anyway. It seemed our ladies' man was also a drug dealer. And he had some prison time to put in.

We parted as friends and he told me that if I ever needed anything, whether it was rent money or advice or a shoulder to cry on, I could count on him. He wrote me while he was away from time to time. But I would tear the letters up. This wasn't the kind of man it made sense for me to sit around waiting for.

Knight had gotten to know Momma before he went away, and they stayed in touch as well. One day I stopped by her house and she told me, "You need to talk to him; he heard you got married and he keeps calling and he wants to talk to you."

He was back home, getting himself together and working a job and trying to stay out of the police's way. I didn't call him. But I *did* end up being there and answering when he called my Momma's phone one day. Knight wanted to know right away if it was really true that I had gotten married already, so soon after breaking up with my son's father. He was trying so hard to figure it out. Who was this guy? What was his deal? Would the marriage last? Since the last time we had talked, Knight had gotten his financial house in order. He had taken care of business. It all sounded so good. But I was a married woman, so I wished him well and I said goodbye.

Years later, after my divorce, Knight and I reconnected. I had moved out of Momma's by then. Now I was into my lower-level rental home, with my two children sharing a room because it was all I could afford at the time. Sitting at a table at work with my friend, I just up and decided to send him a Facebook message. He called right away and wanted to talk.

"Want to talk to a friend? You want to go eat or something?"
And we never separated from that day. It's been nine years.

OUR BEST VERSIONS

When Knight and I reconnected, I was not managing my
expenses well. I was going through a divorce and I was jug-
gling money by paying down one bill one month, another bill
the next. But never all the bills every month. He looked at my
shortfalls and started asking how much I needed each month.
This man had no responsibility to me or my children, but he
wanted genuinely to help me improve my financial situation.
Each Friday he would ask me what I needed and give me it right
out of his paycheck. "As long as I've got enough money to get
gas and drive to work," he told me one month, "I've got what I
need." It was an exaggeration, of course, but he was that committed to helping me improve. The bogus cable I was paying
$20 a month for also had to go, he thought. If I couldn't afford
to buy cable the right, legal way, I didn't need to have cable,
he told me one afternoon. And I couldn't argue with his logic.

And just like that, I started paying all the bills on time. His
financial help was a boost. His inspiration lifted me up even
more and showed that he was as committed to my financial
health makeover as I was. I started to be able to picture a
future with this man where we could count on each other,
and work in tandem toward a shared set of financial goals,
not just each go off and work on our own.

I said, "You know what? I'm gonna get with a credit consol-
idator next."

OUR FIRST HOME

We dated for three years before we got married. You read
that right. This time I took it nice and slow. In all honesty, I
dragged my feet.

Knight would ask me if I would marry him, and I would say,
"No, I'm not getting married again. It's overrated." And part
of me truly thought that I wouldn't marry again. I wasn't
trying to be a two-time divorcee. And that couldn't happen
if I never got married again, right? It's flawless logic, really.

And yet, I'm a church girl at heart. My Godly thoughts of
shacking up and living in sin started to play in my mind,
and when he bought a ring, took me to his mom's, and in
front of her got on his knees and asked me to marry him
again, I said, "Yes." Knight was just so happy to ask me that
I thought to myself, *How could this be?* It seemed like God
was giving me everything my heart desired constantly. How
was this possible? We were having so much fun together, and
on every other Sunday he and I would go to church to give
our time to God. Knight told me, "You know, I never really
went to church before I got with you."

My mother preached to us all the time before she passed

away, telling him to get baptized and let God's blood cover him. One Sunday we woke and gathered the kids and went to church, and Knight just said to me, "I am going to get baptized today." I was in shock and watching God work in his life. My mother was proud of him. And it was one more thing I had prayed for that God had seen fit to deliver.

Even more was close on the horizon, though. Knight and I were soon ready to buy our first home together. This was a real marker of financial security, an accomplishment for us both. And once I knew what it felt like to acquire property, I was hooked! Right away I wanted us to purchase another house that could serve as our first group home.

It took a year for us to gain approval for that loan, and with that we were off and running! I was so excited and immediately I started asking the bank questions. "How do I get another home? Cause I'm thinking about the business plan now."

"Oh, it is going to be about $10,000 down that you'll need for the next one."

So, I told my husband, we have to come up with $10,000 to get another home. So that's what we did a year later; we got another house. And we had built up by now a steady stream of referrals from my prior employers. God created the space for enough revenue where we could pay our bills and still keep growing. I didn't have to rob Peter to pay Paul anymore.

After we bought our fourth group home, I realized we were buying a new home a year and I wanted to bring all of our residents together under one roof. It's incredible. My husband and I have built a real financial legacy for our children. But what's more impressive to me than the assets is the partnership. My husband saw who I was, with all my flaws, and he wanted to help me to be the best version of myself, even when there was nothing in it for him. And I was able to stand still in my discomfort at baring what I was embarrassed about in my finances with my husband and accept his help and his advice. I didn't close up, run away, and move on.

CHAPTER 10

I Believe in the Survival

"Be unapologetically powerful and brave. Let no one convince you there are limits or boundaries to what you can achieve."

—PASTOR SARAH JAKES ROBERTS

I don't think of my story as a sad one. Yes, there's some bad stuff in there. Losing my daughter and my mother were incredibly terrible storms to weather. And I wouldn't wish childhood sexual abuse on anyone. But I can't say for one second that I don't love my story. I truly believe that the journey I've been on has delivered me into a life of incredible abundance. I've found financial freedom with a man who is my true partner. What may be most special about my story is its power to bless other women. God has shown me how my story of love, growth, strength, and success can help other women who are walking through the darkest parts of their journeys.

And I feel particularly called to reach a hand out to mothers whose own trauma history may have made them worried about protecting their own daughters, or those who worry that if they're called to help their child through the horrors of sexual abuse, they may not be up to the task.

GOOD WORK, MOMMA

I told you early in this book that I don't like when people pile on my mom. I was sensitive to that before I ever put pen to paper to start writing. I've been thinking a lot about how I can hand you these memories of my mom without it coming across that she wasn't an amazing mother.

Because she was. She was doing the job of two parents, for eleven children, living in poverty, and dealing with failing health. And she turned out eleven children who are educated, productive citizens and loving children of God. She did her work.

But there are also things that I've learned from what I didn't get in childhood. And I feel called to share those lessons with you. I think about what my mom would tell me if I could have a two-sided conversation with her about how I tell you about her parenting. I know that she would say to do what I need to do. She would ask me, "Just don't go at me too hard, Tiyah."

So, I'm going to tell you how I think it happened that I got assaulted. I don't know that anything could have prevented it. I'm just not sure. But I can point out for you, and for me, the places where I see that maybe things weren't as safe as they could have been for me as a little girl.

I believe that her toughness made her believe that nobody would try anything with her children. She just didn't let it enter her mind. It is an ugly thought to live with. What I would tell Momma if I could go back in time and what I tell myself on a daily basis is that we just have to be a little more cautious about who we leave our children with. If that means we have to miss a night of going out with our friends in order to not just drop them off with anybody, that's okay. Or it might mean not being able to do night school in person but having to do it online. Or maybe it affects the way you're going to plan your work hours and the advancement you're going to be able to put yourself up for at a given time. I can't make all of those decisions for you. And I'm for sure not here to tell you that you should be limiting the dreams that you're going to go after when it comes to education or work simply because you are a mother. But I am here to tell you that it has to be in your mind.

Something could still happen. At a certain point you have

to ask God to come in and put it in His hands. But first, you need to do your work to see if this is the right decision.

LAYING THE FOUNDATION

What would have made me say something as soon as it happened? What would have made me know that I could trust or tell my mom right away? I just don't know.

I try to talk to my daughter about it constantly, and I say, "You know that you should never let anyone touch your privates; that's your private area and that's sacred only for you."

I also tell her, "If someone does something, it's never your fault, okay? Even if you have not told me and you've been holding it. You're never in trouble for something like that because you are a child, you know?"

When my mom told me, "Don't let anyone do this," she didn't mean that it would be my fault. But I misinterpreted because it was so broad and she delivered her words with that force. "Well, you know you better tell me if someone ever touches you there."

That was her way of making sure I understood I needed to come to her. But at the moment when it happened, I didn't even understand what had happened to me. By the time I realized that I should tell, I believed I had waited too long and would get in trouble for not telling sooner. I still wondered if it was my fault that I didn't prevent it.

I want my daughter to be armed with so much assurance from me that there is no way that either her own worry or a predator could make her believe that if something happened, it was her fault. That's the way a predator takes away your protection from your child. By making them believe that you will not believe them or that you will blame them. So, you have to safeguard that in advance. You have to solidify that relationship with your child long before anything ever happens so there is no room where guilt or worry or lies from a predator can get in between you and them. You have to build that closeness and then just again and again knit it closer and closer together. And you have to do it with softness, kindness, communication, and assurance.

Let them know that you love them and will always be there for them to talk to. Tell them they can always say, "Mom, I want to talk to you by myself," and you find time for that. And find time for it in advance, regularly.

The other thing I make sure to say to my daughter in different ways is, "I trust you. I trust you to make good decisions. And I trust you to include me on things in your life."

I tell her, "When you are having doubts, come to me because that's what I'm here for. I'm not asking for you to include me because I don't trust you. I'm asking because you're not in this alone. God gave you a mother because He wants you to have backup until you are grown."

LIVING THAT TRUTH

It's not enough, though, for us to teach our daughters—and our sons and ourselves—about protecting our bodies, though. We're all on a journey to learn about how we can protect our hearts and our power.

The #MeToo movement has helped with this, but we need to do more. I am exhausted from telling my story to a group of women and having every person in the room respond with their own tale of abuse—mental, sexual, physical. We have all come of age in a culture that asks women to give up their power and to ignore the small and large ways that our bodies and our boundaries are encroached upon. It's time for that to stop. I am proud to be living at a time when this country is starting to realize how much the disenfranchisement of women damages us all.

The recovery of what author Iyanla Vanzant calls fatherless daughters is also work that our whole country needs to do. My mother was one of those fatherless daughters, and I was, too. I love my father, and I'm so glad that he remains in my life to this day. But coming up, he wasn't in my home. He wasn't there for his little girl every night at dinner. Momma, of course, never even knew her daddy. Iyanla tells us that sent us both out in the world looking for men to fill the hole left by not having our fathers. The joke was on us, though, because we didn't have present fathers. So, we were flying blind in those relationships with men, trying to replace something we had never even known.

I have been discriminated against because I started so young, because I'm a woman, and because I'm black. Now, owning real estate, when different people come in, they often want to know who built this business and how. I can tell the ones who are happy for me and plan on helping me grow this empire. And I can tell the ones who are going to be trouble and try to find fault in the young black girl's business. So, I have to fight harder to stay in the race. I am a woman. And I'm a black woman. And sometimes it does get hard. Having diversity in our organization is important to me. There are so many different gifts and talents we all bring to the table. It's certainly been my experience that not everyone shares my sentiments. You can tell who is who really quickly when asking people to work with a new black company.

That's when God shows up, though, and sends people in higher places—people such as bankers, accountants, investors—from all backgrounds, who are ready to love you and your business no matter what color your skin is. They believe in the dream drive and the vision. Numbers don't lie, and when you have the organization of your business together and are doing what God has called you to do, He will bless you right in front of the ones who thought they were too good to work with you.

My company, Cache James Better Living, will continue to grow its organization. And there will be a few people who will wish they would have stepped in and been a part of our success. Opportunities, jobs, and retirement funds will be built right here for the community of people who want to get involved and help us reach unimaginable goals. For those who never discriminated against us: thank you. For those who have been a part of the journey: thank you. Let's continue to make history. Thank you, Jesus!

Some people worry about the future, but I am nothing but optimistic. Look at what we've been able to weather over the past year! I see so much strength in our country, even during the pandemic, the way we are overcoming, breaking barriers, and persevering.

In fact, I spent my entire life searching for the Holy Spirit and ended up finding him at home in my living room in the middle of the pandemic! He is awesome and if you seek him wholeheartedly you shall find him.

CHAPTER 11

The Vision

"A woman who walks in purpose doesn't have to chase people or opportunities. Her light causes people and opportunities to pursue her."

—BISHOP T.D. JAKES

I told you earlier that even though I wasn't yet born when she went to Heaven, I've always loved my sister who died when she was a baby. She was one of the people whom I would call for when I was really hurting. Somehow, I knew that she was one of my angels up there who was available to comfort me, always looking out for me. I credit my mom for making me understand so deeply at that young age that the people who are part of our family are never really gone from us. I knew I was always in the company of angels before I even reached double digits!

Now, we're fast-forwarding to years and years later, and in

one of the most important moments of my life God knew to weave two things into it that have always been so special to me: my sister and numbers. I've always been nuts for numbers. My lucky number is eleven (clock this chapter number, if you will…) and I have other numbers that, when I see them, I know they have meaning for me. And birth dates are part of that as well. That's how I know it was no accident that God gifted me with the Holy Spirit on my sister's birthday, even though I didn't realize it until after the fact.

On that day, I had called my sisters over. From 2019 into 2020, I had seen the numbers eleven and forty-four everywhere. Seriously. When I tell you that these numbers were showing up like mad, it was to the point where my husband and I had started joking that we were going to win the lottery. That's how often God was showing these numbers to us at that moment in time. Every time something good happened, I would see these numbers.

But as it kept happening, it started to make sense. Here were the angels talking to me in my language—in numbers— because they knew that I would be able to hear it. They were saying, "You're in the right place at the right time. Things are going to be happening and you're alive and living at the right time."

It started to feel very clear to me that something big was on the horizon, but I felt the presence of those angels and so

I wasn't scared. I wasn't totally peaceful about it, though! I was ready, looking everywhere trying to see what these signs were leading me to, preparing me for. Then as 2020 started, Oprah Winfrey announced she was going on tour...

Oprah announced in her magazine in January that she would be hitting the road, doing arena-sized events in nine cities for what she was calling Oprah's 2020 Vision: Your Life in Focus. I told my friends, "This is it. We're going." And whether they believed me or not that this was the event I had been called to, I think they just always want to be a part of what's going on in my head because they've seen over time that when I feel God speaking to me, something good is going to come out of it! So, they were all like, "We're in!"

I said what if we all shared a room! We bought tickets, got to New York, and I told my friends and sister, "I'm not trying to tell you all what to do, but I'm sitting on the floor. I came out here and I'm hoping to see up close and personal."

One of my friends joined me and I said as we were getting settled in, "What if Oprah comes to our aisle?" You know what happened. Oprah ended up coming right there to our aisle. I was three people from the end, and I took a picture of her right there. I was in awe. My mom just adored Oprah, and here I am three people away from this woman whom my mom had raised me on, and I was starstruck. But then, also, I am always prepared. I do my homework. And Oprah had given us all an assignment in preparation for her Vision Tour, play. So, you know I had done my assignment.

As I came down from that high, I quickly flipped my phone so that I could send this photo of Oprah and me to my sister who was up in the seats, and I saw the time. You guys, it was 11:44. The moment I met Oprah Winfrey was 11:44. Clearly this was what all those elevens and fours had been calling me to, right?

PRESENTS

2020 VISION:
YOUR LIFE IN FOCUS

The day was incredible, and I was riding high as we headed home from New York. I didn't have a lot of time to come down, though, as just the next month I was preparing to leave for a conference with Bishop T.D. Jakes. He's one of the pastors I grew up watching on television; my mom and I both loved him. And at the same point that I had registered for Oprah's tour, I had also heard that Pastor Jakes would be doing this conference. I was so thirsty for the knowledge that I knew he was going to share. It was like my soul was hungry for it. So, I was ready to go, but, of course, the pandemic had other plans. My husband and I were getting set to attend this conference together and then we heard it was canceled. As March bled into April, church was also closed down. I had been thirsting for this spiritual learning and interaction, and now left and right opportunities to fellowship were being taken away.

We decided to open up our living room to a close circle for worship, and a realtor that I work with called me because she now had seen me in my church element and she said that there was someone I reminded her of and that I should look her up. Her name was Pastor Sarah Jakes Roberts. I did, and it changed my life. What do you know, this is Pastor Jake's daughter! And she's wonderful. We started watching her weekly, all through that spring and summer.

During that time, I gave up drinking. I had never been a big drinker, but as I was spending more and more time that summer with Pastor Jakes and in prayer, it felt like I wanted to give more of my undivided attention to God and to my family and my work. So, I gave that up.

Now July comes along, and I hear that Pastor Sarah Jakes is having a virtual conference, and I know that I need to be there. I reach out to my sisters, my friends, and I tell them all that they need to be there. I invited just my sisters to participate in the conference from my house, though, because I knew they were completely spiritually walking with God at this time and I wanted them around me, to help me understand the shift in my life that's was taking place.

The day of the event arrived, and it's as amazing as I hoped it would be. We're five hours in and having these incredible conversations. We're so deep into prayer and I look at the clock and I see that it's just reached 11:44. Here I am so dropped deeply into prayer and that's the time that I see on the clock, 11:44. I looked at my sister Precious and she said, "You know if you ask Him for it, He will give it to you." I didn't ask her who or what she meant, because in that moment I knew she meant God almighty would give me the presence of the Holy Spirit. I stood up and started my worship.

I felt myself standing up and I raised my hand and I started praising God, like I do on Sundays when I'm at home. I'm not going to lie to you, though, during those other times when I've been moved to stand, it's passion that I've felt. But before that day I had not been touched by the Holy Spirit. I raised my hands and I started saying, "Oh, thank you, Jesus."

I kept talking, praising, but the words were floating off my tongue. I wasn't even aware of forming these words, I just felt them coming out. I was praying for about an hour and nothing happened. I had dropped to my knees at some point and now I realized that they were hurting. So, I stood back up and I started thinking about my nephew who was just shot in Chicago a week before, that was my prayer transition. I started crying and I just started thanking God. I said, he could have been gone. We could have been at a funeral this weekend, but you said different. "Thank you. Thank you, Jesus. Thank you."

My older sisters were also in prayer and my oldest sister walked over to me and put her hands on my lower back and on my stomach. In that moment I pointed to the ceiling. I didn't open my eyes, but I looked up inside my mind. And when I looked up to my ceiling, my ceiling became clouds. I fell to the floor. I could not control myself. My hallelujahs were cut in half. I could not complete them anymore. The Holy Spirit was traveling through my body and I was no longer the one in control.

As I came out of this experience, I realized my shirt was soaking wet. I was so drained and sweaty; my face was a mess. But I knew in that moment that I had been touched by the Holy Spirit.

I was so lifted that as soon as my sisters left, I ran to my son's room to let him know that no matter how far God feels, away always know that he is real and he has Mighty Morphing powers! He hugged me, probably just because he could see the delight in my eyes. I was delighted; I was very happy to share this moment with my son. But I also didn't need him to fully understand the moment I was having. It was an angelic, divine moment where God made it clear that I need no one else's approval. He approves of me right where I am right now. That was the gift He gave me when He blessed me with his presence.

This spiritual Journey has me in the best place I have ever been in my life. I have learned that no matter what, I need to remember to include God in every decision. When I do, clarity and discernment powers are the result. In this business, I realized I have to keep Jesus first because he will fight my battles for me.

Conclusion

God called me to share my story with you. He asked me to put it in your hand as a balm to soothe the suffering you're feeling. And he told me it also may serve as a tincture to prevent more pain. It's my hope that what you've read helps you let go of some of the burdens you carry from the past and focus smartly on how to make the future brighter and safer for you and your entire family.

When purpose shows up some people may disappear and some may come back around once they see change can be permanent. I believe in the higher power of God and he showed me how to live in poverty and how to live in wealth. So, I want to be clear: If it all fails, I have the advantage of knowing that I can navigate this world with or without money. Material things and running everywhere people tell you to go do not create the ideal life. Knowing who gives you life and starting to honor that with your whole heart is what creates an ideal life.

One of the biggest lessons I didn't learn in childhood that I've had to learn as a grown-up is that women deserve a real partner in their families and children need to see that partnership in order to know that it's what they should expect as an adult. That doesn't mean that we should judge our fellow humans who are still finding their way there. I inherited my mom's ways, and I don't waste my time judging her choices or my own. I refocus that energy into being fully awake and present in the lives of my children to protect them and build relationships that are solid.

I am proud, too, that I have learned finally that instead of scratching that itch for a new love, I can sit still and wait. I can remember what I appreciate about my husband. I can commit to being vulnerable, scared, and tired, yet still stay. And I can think about the potential risks brought by every new man that might be introduced into my children's lives.

I know that it's not enough to tell my kids that releasing secrets feels amazing and is the key to growth. I have to show by example, like my own mother did. That is part of the reason I've written this book.

I also try to model for my children the attitude of hope and positivity that helped see me through the poverty and chaos of my own childhood. I show them that seeking everyone's approval by compromising your boundaries gains you nothing. Still, I also try to let my children see me leaning away from judgment of others who don't hold their boundaries firm. I've been there, too, and I know that our mistakes of the past can't drag us down—unless we let them.

One of the most important lessons I've learned on motherhood is that being a teen mother means holding two truths in your hand at the same time: 1) It would be better if I had waited to become a mom and 2) It's okay that I didn't wait to become a mom; there's no shame in that path and my child will still have a good parent even though she is young.

I hope that the time you've spent with my story will cause you not just to think differently, but to take action as well. When you are finished reading this book, I hope that if you need to, you'll find a trusted friend (husband, family member, clergy) who will create a safe space for you to free yourself from the secret or secrets you have been holding. Holding that can cause stress and anxiety throughout your life. It might also make you vulnerable to being taken advantage of. Releasing is good for the soul. You can still remain imperfectly perfect...

Next, if you have a daughter, my wish is that you'll start engaging in real, nonthreatening girl talk. Do this to protect them against potential abuse, but also to plan for what you hope will never happen. You want to gain their trust so that they will come and tell you if they're ever abused.

Finally, I hope you'll plan to build something for yourself and your family that will create financial independence. Identify those passions and talents that have been a pattern in your life. Then figure out how to leverage them.

As you finish up reading this book, you now know who I really am; you know where I come from, what I came through, and see that with God's grace I have been able to not live through it, but to build a beautiful family and a legacy for them in the form of a million-dollar business and a solid relationship. And, if I've done it, my sister, trust me when I tell you that you can, too.

I can now add becoming a published author to the list of things that I'm proud of accomplishing, things that probably no one thought I was going to do. I can't wait to hand a copy of this book to my siblings and to my husband. And I can't wait for the first time I hear each of my kids say, "Oh, yeah, my mom wrote a book."

But I also can't wait to hear what *you've* got to say. You can reach me at AtiyahNichols.Afh@gmail.com if you want to share your thoughts on this book and your stories with me. And you can do another thing for me, too.

Now that you're through with the book, I wonder: can you think of anyone you might want to share it with?

You know it wasn't smooth sailing for me. And I know it hasn't been for you. Who else in your life needs to hear that God has plans for her well beyond the hurt she's already lived through?

Hand her my book and tell her, "This girl Atiyah, she started from poverty and she made it, through two marriages, being pregnant at seventeen, into a great life. She's one of us, and she made it, and we can, too."

As my mom used to say, "I don't know what the future holds for us, but I do know who holds the future."

Thank you, Jesus!

Speak loudly, wake up, and dream.

14103714R00114